THE MEME HUMANOIDS

MODERN MYTHS OR REAL MONSTERS

LON STRICKLER

BEYOND THE FRAY

Publishing

ISBN 13: 978-1-954528-30-7

Cover design: Disgruntled Dystopian Publications

Beyond The Fray Publishing, a division of Beyond The Fray, LLC, San
Diego, CA
www.beyondthefraypublishing.com

BEYOND THE FRAY

Publishing

In grateful memory of Rosemary Ellen Guiley, Jc Johnson, Chris Holly and Jodi Polos

CONTENTS

ACKNOWLEDGMENTS

I want to thank the following friends and colleagues for their contributing research, investigations, and assistance. They include, and are not limited to:
The members of Phantoms & Monsters Fortean Research, Butch Witkowski, Stan Gordon, Jamie Brian, Albert S. Rosales, Tobias Wayland, Manuel Navarette, Ken Pfeifer, as well as all the eyewitnesses and the "Phantoms & Monsters" readers. Special thanks to Vincent Richardson for his illustrations.

Please be aware that a few of the eyewitness accounts in this book are written by ordinary people. Some text has been changed; but in some instances, it's been left unedited and as received. Thanks for your understanding.
Lon Strickler

www.phantomsandmonsters.com

INTRODUCTION

THE NEXUS OF THE MEME HUMANOIDS

Throughout the world, but more frequently in North America, people have reported encounters with freakish pale humanoid creatures that have no taxonomic classification. Most anomalous beings, or cryptids, have long been a part of regional folklore. For example, the Mothman of Point Pleasant, West Virginia, and the Beast of Bray Road in Walworth County, Wisconsin, are legendary cryptids associated with specific locations. During the past two decades, a new type of unknown humanoid cryptid has emerged. These sightings are a specific form of mythology that follows the earlier emergence of native tradition and indigenous lore. These humanoids develop from a unique mixture of urban legend that has its origins on the internet. This fictional, viral monstrosity is referred to as "Creepypasta."

So what are these Creepypastas? It is a phenomenon that proliferates across the internet to such an extent that each creation has developed into its digital myth. Instead of transmitting by word of mouth, these tales spread via chain emails, online forums, and websites designed specifically for their promulgation. The most well-known Creepypasta is the narrative of "Slenderman," a tall, thin, faceless, black-suit-clad man who preys on unsuspecting children. The Slenderman was concocted on June 10, 2009, by a Japan-based American expatriate for an internet Photoshop contest. Images depicting this imaginary entity and affiliated backstory began to circulate throughout various online forums, and in quick order, the Slenderman meme went viral. Imaginative internet users began to expand on the Slenderman myth and formulated entire stories around it. The Slenderman was transformed into a modern-day boogeyman.

In a 2012 interview for BBC Radio 4, the Slenderman creator, Eric Knudson, observed that "even though people realize that Slenderman was created on an internet forum in June 2009, some still believe that he might be real." Two years later, this bizarre reality made international headlines when two teenage girls from Waukesha, Wisconsin, stabbed their friend nearly to death because of their imagined illusion that their crime would earn them a place in Slenderman's presumed mansion in the woods.

The Slenderman is not the only Creepypasta humanoid to break out from the internet and unfold itself in the material world. Another virtual creation that makes its appearance known is a humanoid referred to as "the Rake." The Rake myth emerged in 2005 when an anonymous poster on the imageboard website 4Chan decided to create a contemporary monster. The poster described their brainchild as "Humanoid, about six feet tall when standing, but usually crouches and walks on all fours. It has very pale skin. The face is blank. As in, no nose and no mouth. However, it has three solid green eyes, one in the middle of its forehead, and the other two on either side of its head, towards the back. When it attacks, a mouth opens, as if a hinged skull that opens at the chin. Reveals many tiny, but dull teeth." This creature, which is believed to have been inspired by the so-called "crawlers" from the 2005 horror film *The Descent*, evolved throughout the 4Chan thread. The monstrous humanoid gradually transformed into a gaunt, naked, pale-skinned, humanlike creature that crawls on four long spindly limbs. This entity was thus dubbed "the Rake." It would be several years before the concept of the Rake gained traction in the Creepypasta community.

In December 2008, user posts featuring this made-up Rake humanoid appeared on the Russian social networking site Live-Journal. In April 2009, the Rake humanoid returned to 4Chan, its birthplace. In a matter of a few months, the Rake made its way onto SomethingAwful.com, where it served as an inspiration for Eric Knudson's Slenderman. By 2010, the legend of the Rake was quickly spreading throughout the internet, pervading all manner of Creepypasta websites, evolving into fan art and creative fiction, which added intensity and color to its mythos.

In 2012, an incredible phenomenon began to occur. Internet users, in earnest, began reporting frightening encounters with emaciated, pale, hairless humanoids that, for the most part, crawled on all fours. Internet users attempted to equate these entities with characters of Native American mythology, oblivious to the fact that the humanoids in these encounters bore a resemblance to the fictional Rake. Many witnesses suggested that they were "Skinwalkers," medicine men or witches of traditional Navajo lore who possess the ability to transform into animals. Others proposed that these emaciated humanoids were manifestations of the "Wendigo," a malevolent cannibalistic spirit of Cree and Algonquin legend. Others still began to invent new names for these creatures, such as "Flesh-gaits" and "Crawlers," the latter evoking the 2005 movie entities that likely helped to inspire the Rake originally.

The vast number of reliable witnesses who claim to have seen these humanoids, coupled with the fact that many of these witnesses appear to be ignorant of the urban legends, suggests two interesting possibilities. Namely, that the creator of the Rake meme unconsciously contrived an entity that previously existed, or that the human imagination or subconscious continuously materializes these beings into reality. This phenomenon is known as thought-form or tulpa manifestation. If this is the case, then one must ask, "What came first – the monster or the myth?"

The term "thought-form" describes the concept of an entity created directly and exclusively by the mind, whether unconsciously or consciously. These entities appear to develop a life of their own, a distinct being that is perceptible to other people. The belief in thought-forms is the basis of several concepts throughout history, specifically the "tulpa" in Tibetan tradition, the "pooka" in Germanic and Celtic cultures, and the "djinn" in Arabic belief. Early records of Western explorers experienced an embodied form of consciousness as benign beings that accompanied them and, in some cases, befriend them. More recently, poltergeist manifestations have been attributed to a thought-form.

It does seem that consciousness, as the result of various experiments and trials, can partition and extend itself beyond the human mind. This provides a context for understanding reported psychokinetic phenomena, notably apparitional appearances, and additional unexplained manifestations.

The humanoid encounters and sightings that are detailed in this book offer varied glimpses into the phenomenon. Ask yourself – are these humanoids actual corporeal beings that are manifested by the human mind and perceivable by others? Or are we witnessing the nexus of an unknown and monstrous species of humanoid?

GREY ALIENS, WALKERS, AND CRAWLERS

During the years following World War II, there was an increase of unidentified flying object sightings and, eventually, the advent of alien beings who were supposedly piloting these otherworldly craft. As time went on, these beings were designated as "Grey Aliens" or simply "Greys."

The origins of the Greys may go back to an earlier time. In the 1890s a few novels began to describe encounters with small, grey-skinned alien races with oversized balloon-shaped heads. Author H. G. Wells later predicted humanity's future appearance as evolved humanoids with diminished mouths and noses, no hair, and with large heads. The Morlocks and the Eloi were examples of Wells' successor species to humanity.

The perceived existence of these beings would occasionally make their way into our culture as having freakishly large heads in proportion to their bodies. These descriptions included a hairless body and no noticeable outer ears or noses, sometimes with small orifices for ears, nostrils, and mouths. In drawings, Greys were usually shown with very large, opaque, black eyes. They were frequently described as shorter than average adult humans.

The Greys were later linked to the alleged crash-landing of possibly more than one alien craft in the desert surrounding Roswell, New Mexico, in 1947. A few publications contained statements from individuals who claimed to have seen US military personnel in the possession of unusually shaped, bald, child-sized humanoids.

As time progressed, the descriptions of these humanoids would vary a bit. But existence theories have continued to evolve, especially in those literary accounts that described close encounters and possible human abduction.

It's not my intent to argue the theories pertaining to the Grey Aliens or any other supposed extraterrestrial faction. I simply want to establish a base as to how the grey and/or pale humanoids have been depicted in the past.

There is one account that, I believe, serves as a good starting point for the advent of the modern-era humanoids. The Dover Demon is a small humanoid reportedly observed in Dover, Massachusetts. It was the subject of a profound panic during the 1970s, when multiple witnesses came forward with their sightings. The Dover Demon is described as looking sort of like a "Grey Alien," except that it has skin of a rosy orange instead of opaque gray. The Dover Demon has a large head on a demure, spindly body. It can be bipedal, but it often moves as a quadruped and switches back and forth between the two modes of locomotion. It has eyes that seem to glow, alternating between orange and green. The body appears to be nude without any covering.

It seems that sightings only occur during a brief period, though the number of sightings in recent years have been scattered at best.

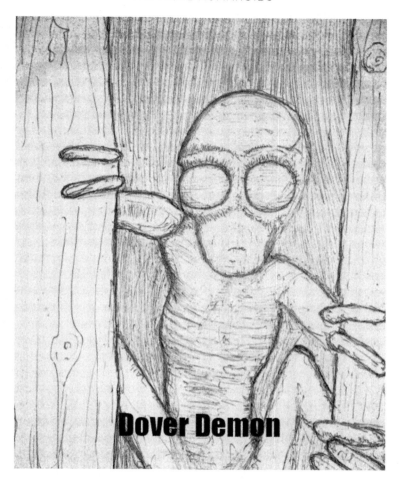

Dover Demon

The initial sighting was reported to be at 10:32 p.m. on April 21, 1977, as three seventeen-year-olds, Bill Bartlett, Mike Mazzocca and Andy Brodie, were traveling north on Farm Street. Bartlett, the driver of the Volkswagen, observes something creeping along a low wall of loose stones on the left side of the road. At first, he believes the figure is a dog or a cat until his headlights shine on it. He then realizes that he's looking at an entity that he has never seen before. The figure slowly turns its head and stares into the light. The two large, circular, lidless eyes shine brightly "like two orange marbles." Its watermelon-shaped head, resting at the top of a thin neck, is the size of the rest of its body. Except for its oversized head, the creature is extremely thin, with long spindly arms and legs, and large hands and feet. The skin is hairless and peach-colored and appears to have a rough texture. "Like wet sandpaper," Bartlett subsequently describes the skin of the being. Standing no more than three and a half to four feet in height, the figure is shaped like "a baby's body with long arms and legs." It had been making its way along the wall, its long fingers curling around the rocks, when the car lights captured and surprised it.

Unfortunately, neither of Bartlett's companions observes the unusual being. The sighting lasts only a few seconds, and before Bartlett can speak, the car travels past the scene. Bartlett drops his friends off and quickly drives home. Visibly upset, he walks through the door. His demeanor raises an alarm from his father, who inquires further. Bartlett relates the story and later sketches what he's seen.

Later that same night, at around midnight, fifteen-year-old John Baxter leaves his girlfriend Cathy Cronin's house at the south end of Miller High Road. Baxter starts walking up the street on his way home. Half an hour later, after he has walked about a mile, he observes someone approaching him. Because the figure is short, Baxter assumes it's an acquaintance of his, M. G. Bouchard, who lives on the street. John calls out, and there is no response. Baxter and the figure continue to approach each other until finally the latter stops. Baxter then halts as well and asks, "Who is that?" He can only see a shadowy form. Baxter takes one step forward, and the figure scurries off to the left, running down a shallow wooded gully and up the opposite bank. As the figure runs, Baxter hears its footsteps on the dry leaves. He follows the figure down the slope, then stops and looks across the gully. There, he sees the creature standing in silhouette about thirty feet away, its feet "molded" around the top of a rock several feet from a tree. The creature's body reminds Baxter of a monkey's, except for its dark figure-eight-shaped head. Its two bright eyes are looking straight at Baxter, who after a few moments begins to feel uneasy. Realizing he has never seen such a being before and fearing what it might do next, he backs carefully up the slope. He then "walks very fast" down the road to the intersection at Farm Street. There, a couple passing in a car pick him up and drive him home.

Several years later, a reliable witness in Barnstable Village, on Cape Cod, Massachusetts, states that he had a similar encounter in 1977. He said that at the time he was working at a restaurant in Yarmouth Port, the next town over. He was giving a fellow employee a ride home when they detoured to a beach parking lot to drink a beer after work. It was early summer, around 9:30 at night.

The road was located north of Route 6A, Scudder Lane, and as they were heading back to the main road, they saw something very similar to what is being described as the Dover Demon. It crossed the road in front of them, causing the witness to suddenly apply the brakes to avoid a collision. Although they only saw it for a few seconds in the headlights, it did not attempt to scurry away like a wild animal. In fact, the being slowly and deliberately continued across the road, focusing its stare at the witnesses in the car. The driver described it as three to four feet in height, even though it was walking on all fours. It had a large head in relationship to its body, and the eyes were very prominent since they were large and glowing from the reflection of the headlights.

He states that they were dumbfounded and were at a loss to identify what they had just seen. It seemed apelike because of its stature, but the eyes did not resemble any animal they had ever seen. They only mentioned the encounter to a few friends and family and never reported the incident to any authorities. The driver said that he knows what he saw was real, and perhaps he should have documented it a little more thoroughly.

In late summer 2012, I began to receive reports concerning a bizarre entity that witnesses had encountered in various locations within California's Sierra Nevada Mountains. As time went on, and after I had talked to a few local park rangers, it became evident that a pale white humanoid was making itself known. The initial account I received on August 28, 2012, was, I believe, the nexus for the "Penelope" sightings.

"Sir – my brother referred your email address to me. He thought you may have an answer to what I saw this past July while camping in the Sierra Nevada Mountains near Tioga Lake, CA. My teenage son and I were camping in our RV. There were other campers in the area but not very close to us. On the 3rd night of our trip, we encountered something that neither of us can explain.

This is bear country and I know that there have been Bigfoot reports over the years. But what we saw was neither as far as we can tell. We secured all the food and other supplies in the RV and were getting ready to go to bed. It was about 12:30 am. My son fell asleep quickly while I was getting a few things ready as we were going to leave this location later in the morning. I was looking at a map when I started to hear high-pitched screams. At first, I thought it was a coyote, but it was a single scream and sounded more human, like a woman's scream. I opened the RV door and stood silent in the doorway. Once again, the high-pitched scream started. This time, it woke my son. We both stood at the door as the screams continued from the direction of the mountain. After about 10 mins the screams stopped, so we both went to bed.

Something startled me while I was sleeping because I woke in a panic. I looked at my watch. It was 2:40 am. Then suddenly that same high-pitched scream erupted outside of the RV. As it started my son jumped out of his rack and fell to the floor. I grabbed my .44 just in case. As we looked out through the windshield the moonlight was bright enough to illuminate a tall thin creature with light-colored skin. My son yelled 'zombie!' It did look like a female human form, but the face and the rest of the body looked horrible. It reminded me of an old witch. It had no clothes, a deformed face, long light-colored hair, long arms, and legs. I figured it stood almost 7 ft. It was walking away from the RV toward the lake. I had seen enough. I made sure everything was ready to go and drove out of there ASAP.

We ended up near Mono Lake. A few days later I was able to talk to a ranger as he walked through the camping area. He was an older guy and quite engaging. I described what we witnessed. My son also verified what we had seen. The ranger got a serious look on his face and said that over the years, something similar had been reported a few times. He said that they called it 'Penelope' but he didn't know why it had gotten that name. That's all he knew.

When I got home, I searched the internet, but no information was available. My brother gave me your email address and said that you may have an idea of what it was. I'd appreciate your help." LR

I later talked to the witness, but there wasn't much more information that he could provide, other than that he thought that he'd observed the humanoid attempt to crawl as it moved away from him and his son.

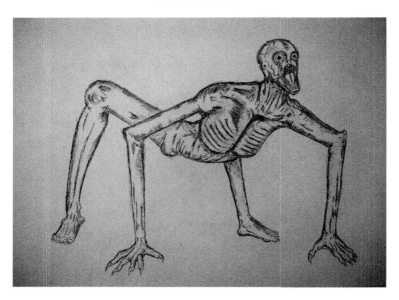

I looked for "Penelope" online. There was one small reference but little detail. I contacted Inyo National Forest for information. They directed me to the Mono Lake ranger station. I was able to talk to a ranger who confirmed that there were a few very odd sightings in the Sierra Nevada range and that one of these "beings" was dubbed "Penelope," but he was unaware of how or why the name was given. I sent out a few inquiries to other ranger stations.

A few days later, I received a short email from a folklore writer in Reno, Nevada, who stated that, "Penelope" was supposedly a woman who became lost in the Sierra Nevada Mountains several years ago and eventually became a flesh-eating monster. OK. Seems like we're getting into the urban-legend column on this one. Well, anyway, I continued to make inquiries.

Then several months later, as dumb luck has it, I saw a reference to "Penelope" in a book I had recently received titled

Monster Spotter's Guide to North America. The brief description is comparable to the information that I received from the folklore writer with a few more gruesome details. It seems "Penelope" disembowels her victims before feasting on the remains. As well, she is supposedly responsible for a few unexplained deaths in the Sierra Nevada Mountains. Other than that, I had no idea what LR and his son witnessed.

On September 30, 2013, I received another email report about another pale humanoid sighting in the Sierra Nevada range:

"I was searching for references in the Sierra Nevadas and I came across a story on your page about a creature named 'Penelope.' The entire encounter and creature described by the 'LR' person who sent the original e-mail was something my entire family and myself had witnessed many years ago.

We were camping near Convict Lake, California, but further back in the woods. There were 3 other groups of campers in the campground, and it was late spring. On our second night there, around 1 am, just outside my old Nissan/Datsun 6-pac camper my father, mother, and I heard a very loud scream. Other people in the camp heard it as well because when I looked out the window, I saw lights in all the tents turn on. Following the scream, a second scream came from the hill across the stream. There were 2 of these creatures! A minute or 2 went by and then again, from the same location, we heard another loud blood-curdling scream. It then proceeded to begin running in the direction of the creature across the stream. It must have been large because my dad is 6'4" 300 lbs and could not make the same loud thuds this creature made when running.

We only got a look at part of it as it emerged from the brush when crossing the stream. It was a whitish blur, at least that's what we saw. Even though several campers had weapons, we left right then and there. This was back in 1986. I don't believe in Bigfoot, aliens, etc., but whatever this was, it was real, and it was very large. I will never go camping without at least a shotgun since that incident. Thanks." M

When I first read this account, I thought that this creature was probably a blond-colored Bigfoot. But when I later talked to the witness, he stated that he believed that it was hairless. He also stated that the screams were high-pitched and shrill. I was later contacted by an employee at the Convict Lake Resort who concurred that other campers had reported similar sightings of large ghostly pale entities that moved swiftly through the forest while making hideous ear-piercing screams. Were these Penelope-like humanoids?

Then in January 2016, I received the following report:

"Hello Lon. I have been searching for months to find answers to what it is my wife and I saw near Labor Day 2014 while camping in the eastern Sierras in the Mono Village area. Most websites are just so outlandish and full of people that want to believe in monsters or UFOS it just became frustrating that any hope of putting together the puzzle and maybe learning something from these rare experiences would be lost.

I read the reported sighting of the man and his son seeing a tall skinny witch-looking thing outside his RV in the same region. Also, I was very interested in an article that discussed the Bigfoot problem and how people might be seeing 'Ghosts' of animals from the past. Is this why it's so hard to gather evidence? Maybe they materialize and de-materialize and we are just lucky to be present. This seems like a legitimate explanation to me because the creature I saw running by the road if living, breathing, and hunting in our physical world would send all the people that live in Mono County back to the city once reports came of its appearance.

I have been coming to the same area to camp and fish for over 30 years. The Twin Lakes resort in Bridgeport, CA, right on the CA-Nevada border, about an hour north of Mono Lake. High elevation, tons of wildlife & great fishing. The one-way road up to the Twin Lakes ends at the base of the huge mountain range, north side of Yosemite. My parents brought me when I was 5 and now, I bring them and my family every year, so I am very familiar with the wildlife. On many occasions had up-close experiences with many of its inhabitants. For instance, one time a bear was spooked and backed up into my tent, sending me flying over the other 2 in my tent. I've seen some stuff.

My family loves to fish, mostly catch and release. My favorite pastime is hiking and bird/animal watching. I have developed a keen eye for locating and identifying all types of wildlife. To give you an example of what I have personally seen in this valley – mountain lion, Sierra moose, bald eagle, golden eagle nesting, mountain goats, osprey, king snake – the list goes on. The point I'm trying to make is I've seen every kind of animal in this wilderness, and I have a great knowledge of every other species of animal all over the world. Nature and wildlife have been a life-long interest of mine and have been the subject of much of my art since a child. Knowing the body parts and how they move together has been essential to understanding as an artist. OK now to the sighting.

My wife, stepson, and I were headed to the creek for some daybreak fishing. We left before dawn to get the car parked and walk to the creek. The time must have been close to 5:30 AM and it was still very dark and slight fog. This trip which is about a quarter mile from the cabin to the creek. It is always full of nocturnal animals headed home after raiding the local campgrounds. So, mule deer, black bear, and huge jackrabbits crossing the road is no surprise. Like I have done a hundred times before, keep an eye out, slow down, hit the high beams to illuminate the beasts with eyes reflecting my car lights.

This time my lights caught something crossing the road that did not have reflective nocturnal eyes, so I slowed down immediately to about 20 MPH and tried my best to identify what it was. I was having trouble doing so since the thing was moving very low to the ground. Its belly is just inches from touching the ground. It appeared very pale or white, so I think goat or sheep. I immediately remembered decades ago there had been sheepherders on the side of the hill, but they had been gone for many years. Well, when my high beams hit this thing, it turned its long neck and glared at us and almost shook its head as if it didn't want to be seen at all. At first sight, it was crossing the street almost diagonally headed our way then along the side of the road in our direction. Now my wife had seen it from the start, but I needed extra time so that I could identify it and give her an explanation of what type of animal it was. I asked her, 'What is that?' I just wanted to make sure she was seeing and observing the same thing I was.

Now the first odd thing that I couldn't understand, besides the way it was crawling so low to the ground is, unlike a hunting cat, the legs were all wrong. Its knees seemed to be backward, but it was running on them. My thought was that it was an escaped sheep or goat that had broken knees and it was running for its life because it was moving fast. As it came closer and closer towards us, I could hardly take my eyes off its freaky legs. I still lay awake at night puzzled by how they were working. I've not seen any mammal move this way. The closest thing would be a crab or insect, the front and back legs moved together in unison. There was no bouncing, swaying, galloping, or jumping like that of a mammal. This creature's torso, which was about 4 feet long, stayed straight, low to the ground as its legs/arms did all the work. To me, it looked like a puppet with a marionette moving it along. So unreal and fast with only its arms/legs moving.

By this time my wife could only get out 'what the hell...' as we saw it from maybe 50 yards away to about 20 yards. You could see that it had no fur at all – just pale, sinewy stretched skin over long, skinny well-defined limbs. Its 'broken' knees were long skinny fingers or claws, a foot long or more. The torso was maybe the size of a large goat, but it also had broad shoulders – very human-like. Possibly like this thing normally walks upright. This is what my wife kept pointing out. The shoulders made it look human. All this was freaky but we both stared intensely, to figure out what it was.

As we got closer the face became more and more defined. The first second we laid eyes on it, the face and head did not make sense. This thing looked like it came out of a horror movie – like a space alien creature or humanoid monster. The nose I was looking for was not there – just a flat opening with two nose holes high up on the face. No ears! Just small holes on the side of its head. It had high-brow ridge bones, but the skull did not have a huge human cranium, more like the size of a chimp. It had a large chin that protruded, maybe strong jawbones. But this part I don't get at all. The eyes. I saw these large eye sockets off in the distance, but they never reflected in the light. When we were 10–15 yards away, I only saw sockets and no eyeball, like that of a blind cavefish. Now, this blew me away. How was this thing turning its head to glare at me with no eyes? Was it a ghost? But as it passed us, and I came to a complete stop, I saw it zip into the chaparral and kick up dust.

This thing was flesh and blood. I might add there was no smell or anything else odd that we noticed. I should have taken pictures of the tracks but did not think to do it because I was very puzzled and thought maybe we had witnessed a ghost because of how unreal it appeared. I was also with my family, which I am very protective of. Normally if I had been alone, I would be on the trail. What this thing was doing so close to a campground puzzles me. My wife said, even though I was only thinking it, this thing seemed intelligent and was creeping in the dark – mad at us for discovering it. The mouth was closed but it had tight closed lips that almost seemed to grin. I did not see any teeth, large canine, or flat herbivores. Its skull was that of a predator – not prey – with eye sockets positioned on the front, not the sides. I have seen a great many extraordinary things in my life, so I have learned to be a great eyewitness and not jump to conclusions – only observe, make a note, and then evaluate later. My wife is the biggest skeptic I have ever met, not fully believing the many extraordinary stories I have told. She comes from a lifetime of cold, hard harsh reality – no room for any stretch of the imagination. Well, now she is a believer and is afraid to this day of what is walking around those Sierra Nevada mountains." SM

The "Penelope" sightings may still exist, though it's been several years since I have received a report. But the pale humanoid phenomenon has continued to expand throughout North America and into several other countries. In this book, I will present personal accounts submitted by actual eyewitnesses. It is up to you, the reader, to discern the difference between myth and reality.

2

CONTEMPORARY GHOULS

In Arabic-Persian folklore, the Ghoul or Ghool are said to stalk the deserts and graveyards. The ghouls are known as one of the three types of djinn. They are said to be supernatural creatures capable of assuming different shapes of animals and even beautiful women to entice travelers off the road. Leading them to lost confusion where they make their move to feast on their flesh.

Ghouls in recent history have been reported all over the world. Malaysian sightings resulted in what was described as mass hysteria followed by the cancellation of schools and the calling in of local police, Islamic scholars, and witch doctors in response. This frequently results in several forms of exorcism.

In this chapter, I present modern versions of these entities. Are these supernatural beings, possibly corporeal thought-form manifestations influenced by pop culture, or something completely different?

The following account from October 2014 may seem to represent a typical ghost, but some characteristics suggest a more complex phenomenon:

"Reports of a flesh and blood girl with 'coal-black pits for eye sockets' first emerged in London in the 1980s – but experts now say she is back.

In October 2014, a local paranormal investigator says he has been flooded with reports. One terrified traveler said he and his wife were waiting for the tube with their child when they heard the chilling sound of a little girl giggling in the tunnel.

'To our amazement, a child, no taller than one meter in height appeared as if out of nowhere further up the track in front of us,' he said. 'We stopped dead in our tracks after noticing her eyes had no color.'

The investigator, who did not want to be named, said: 'I have received nine different reports in the last two years from seemingly credible witnesses. During interviews, most of their stories have been very similar.' It comes after a recent surge in reported sightings of screaming black-eyed child manifestations across the UK.

The 2014 ghoul sightings in the London Underground are not the first in the capital. As well as the black-eyed child being spotted in the 1980s, other ghoulish sightings are said to have frequented the tracks of various stations for years."

On June 6, 2016, the following email from a listener was read by the host Dave Schrader on Darkness Radio:

"A while back I was working as a courier for a company. My duties included picking up specimens from the hospital. One morning when I was driving, after picking up specimens from the hospital, I noticed there was a car going in the opposite direction. The car only had one visible person driving the car. She had curly wet brown hair with both of her hands on the steering wheel at the ten and the two o'clock position. We crossed each other's paths going in the opposite directions and now, we as drivers, are parallel to each other. She is on my left side while I am also on her left side. Something made me turn and look and things suddenly went in slow motion.

I saw a person sitting next to her who wasn't there before. It looked like a woman with very dark hair, pale white skin, and dark eye sockets. When we went past each other, I thought, 'Wow, that's weird!' I need to make a U-turn and take a second look.

So, I stop at the nearest light, make a U-turn, and right when I did, now the passenger is on the other side of the street and when the drivers are parallel to each other, things went in slow motion, the passenger with pale white skin with the very dark hair turned and looked at the driver but I think she was looking at me. She still doesn't have any eye sockets, just big open gaping holes. She opened her mouth and all I saw was total darkness in her mouth. Somehow it felt as though she were sucking my soul.

The slow-motion broke and I resumed driving off, almost crashing into traffic mid-section. Reality then hit me, I thought about it and, I just saw something I should not have seen. Question is, what the heck is that thing?"

I received this account from an eyewitness in September 2018:

"Back when I was in high school my friend and I saw something I've begun referring to as a crawler. This was in Rossville, Illinois. Nighttime and in a cemetery. I think it was probably late summer or early fall because I don't remember it being too cold out. Would have been between 2007 and 2010. Pretty sure the moon was full or close to it because visibility was pretty good.

My friend and I used to walk this loop. We would leave her place and go down a block to a side road that led to a park. We would then turn left and cut across the park to the side entrance of the cemetery. The cemetery and park sat at the very southwest corner of town. Beyond that were just woods and cornfields. If we went straight across the cemetery, it would take us to another side road that then led to the main street, back to where her house was.

We made it to the cemetery and were walking the main drive that split the property in half. There was a sudden noise that made us both stop. My friend started laughing nervously and asked if I had heard the noise. I told her I had seen what made the noise.

To our left, I had seen something running behind the headstones. It was on all fours, but humanoid. It had extremely pale skin and no hair and looked very thin. I remember it was so pale it almost reflected the moonlight. It moved so fast (too fast for any human I've ever seen on their hands and feet) that I couldn't see many details. It was in total profile, so I never saw the facial details. The way it ran was animal-like as well in that it had that gait where its feet came forward almost between or past its hands. Watch a video of a big cat or wild dog running to see what I mean.

We were both terrified. We just stood there panicking and listening to it moving around, just out of sight, while we called one of her friends to come to meet us and take us the rest of the way home. Her friend, a very typical high school boy, arrived and naturally wanted to stay in the cemetery and goof off for a while. For some reason with him there acting dumb it was less scary, but I remember it just kept making these wide circles around us. It always stayed out of sight, but you could hear it as it moved. Occasionally it would come a bit closer, then seemed to dart further away again.

Eventually, we left. I spent a while researching it and even reached out to a paranormal group in Champaign for advice. The guy I talked to had never heard of it but wanted to document what we saw. We met up with him and did an interview, but the group never did an investigation.

Fast forward a few years and I'm living in Aurora, Colorado. I met one of my closest friends in about 2012. We hit it off because we were into the paranormal. When I eventually told him about what I had seen, his jaw hit the floor. He told me he had seen the same thing and told me his story.

He described exactly what I had seen, but he had seen it under a porch while living in Thornton. It was crouched down and squatting. He thinks he startled it while it was eating because he said it was hunched over something it was holding. He comes from a Navajo/Apache background, and when we first met, his best guess was Skinwalker. But then and especially now he said he had doubts about either of those things being the answer. He was dating a girl at the time whose mom claimed to be a medium. She said she thought it was something that someone 'woke up' and that now it was angry. We both have serious doubts on that one.

The stranger part came when he and I brought it up. We both started having very intense nightmares about it. His were worse than mine and lasted much longer. This was also punctuated by 6 months filled with a lot of bad luck and anxiety for us. I always sort of brushed this off as us just psyching ourselves out, until I sent my story into a podcast. After it was read, another listener sent in their story. They described what my friend and I had seen and described the sightings as being punctuated by nightmares. I couldn't write that off because he spoke about his nightmares in detail, and they matched my friend's nightmares exactly. I have never given out details of what happened in either of our nightmares.

I've read a ton of other stories by other users and people on the internet. I've dug through mounds of lore and cryptid lists. I still don't feel like I have an answer to what this thing is. My best guess at this point is that the nightmares aren't coincidental and that this is interdimensional. It seems like it can interact with physical things around it, but I've never heard anyone tell a first-hand account of being physically attacked or even touched. I've speculated on what it could be for hours, and the only conclusion that I've come to is that I don't feel like there is an actual concrete answer. It doesn't act exactly like this or that cryptid. I think it might be something that's been around and inspired other cryptids and paranormal tales."

This account brings up another question. Can dreams manifest into corporeal entities? Can a nightmare open a gateway into another world or dimension? I have heard psychic mediums and other gifted persons suggest that it does happen.

In December 2018 I received an interesting email from a truck driver:

"I'm a truck driver and we tend to see some of the most beautiful things this great country has to offer. However, in contrast we see some of the most gruesome, from mangled roadkill to cars and people equally unrecognizable. I will never forget what I saw that night.

I was driving at around 0300 MDT along Wyoming's desolate I-80. That's when a thick fog rolled up on me seemingly out of nowhere and the air was almost electrified. I didn't pay much mind to it at that point. I just slowed down and put on my 4-ways and just kept trucking. That is until I thought I saw a person staggering away from a vehicle broken down on the shoulder. I was about to stop and call 911 when I saw it, a chunk of flesh fell from his pale face. Then he turned and just stared with these bright red eyes. I was going about 5 mph and quickly got it up to 45 mph when I saw another 20 or 30 walking along the interstate, all with these bright red eyes and pale rotten flesh. I didn't dare to stop until I got to Ft. Bridger.

It was then that the fog cleared, and I noticed a US Army convoy braking at the truck stop I was at. They then proceeded out in the direction of what a couple of other truckers told me are known as the Wyoming zombie walkers as they will walk any given stretch of highway or back road in that state, looking for their next human victim.

A lot of weird things out on these roads and any trucker will tell you if you can stay home at night, do it, because you never know what's around that next corner or waiting just beyond the reach of your lights." NG

So, this question begs an answer. What are these humanoids that people refer to as zombies? Film, television, and pop culture are rife with productions centered around these horrific humanoids. There is a long history of zombies in the Americas, but not as pale rotting corpses walking aimlessly about while searching for victims to feed on.

This account was referred to me in August 2020. Two friends from Milwaukee, Wisconsin, are driving at night in an unknown rural area. They encounter two black-eyed kids, and later, they hit an unknown pale grey humanoid on the dark road:

"This encounter happened to me about 12 years ago. I was around 24 at the time. I worked hospitality, so it would be later at night when my friends and I hung out. So, at around 9 o'clock my friend and I decided to go for a drive, someplace we've never been. We just get in the car and go. I offered (and wanted to) drive because my mother was out of town, and I was using her Mercedes. It was one of those early 1990s E bodies, the ones that were big piles of heavy steel, a real tank of a car. I only mention the car body because it becomes relevant later in the story. He happily agreed and we hit the road.

We lived near Milwaukee, Wisconsin, at the time. We drive north out of the city and for about an hour when I see an exit I don't recognize and decide to get off there. There was nothing at this exit other than cornfields, no gas station or restaurant signs, and no visible light of a town in any direction. So, we are in a place we don't recognize but that was the point, just driving to get nowhere because the speed limit was 35 mph, and we were in no rush. The moon was bright enough that everything was visible.

About a mile into the cornfields, we could see 2 kids on the right side of the road. We comment on how weird it is because there is no housing or stores, not even lights on a horizon. Plus, it was 10:30ish at night. We're two larger guys so we don't worry about anything. I slow down so we can inquire if their car broke down or if they were ok.

As we pulled up, I noticed the clothing of the kid in front. It was a stained cream-colored tweed-type shirt with real tattered sleeves and overalls with only one strap. He appeared to be maybe 12 years old. The second kid was taller wearing a red flannel-type shirt, with old-time-looking khaki pants. However, I could barely notice the taller kid standing further behind the smaller one because as I pulled up while noticing the clothes, I got to see the whole 'child' fully and his arms were to his side slightly raised, almost in that iconic zombie way. But his eyes. I couldn't look away, and I did my best to mutter to my friend, 'You're seeing this too, right?' His eyes were pitch black, blacker than the night, but easy to see as he stood there staring at us. I did not know what the heck I was seeing but I've never been so frightened in my life, and I've had several odd experiences that have left me unable to deny that there is more in this world than what we understand. So, we're stopped for a moment locking eyes with whatever this thing was. It was no child, it was evil. I have zero doubts about that.

We quickly agree to go and fast. We are not going to inquire with them. This was straight out of the twilight zone, and I remembered the hitchhiker and that was not happening tonight. No sir! So, we go, and we clamor between ourselves, 'What the $#@& did we just see? What was that, what the hell was that?' Still, no signs of homes, just open cornfields. How could these 2 kids be there? I don't know but I don't believe those were kids.

So, I keep driving, and we get out of the fields into a wooded windy road shortly after around 5 minutes. As I'm driving through a curve going about 45 mph, a creature walks in front of my car. As I saw it, it was nothing like I ever saw. Its spine was tall, it stuck above the hood ornament as I hit it. It was a pale grey color and looked like nothing I've ever seen. It had a very tall arch in its spine, almost like when a cat hisses and goes on its toes, that kind of shape but in a very tall gangly creature. I hit this thing straight on with the Benz. My friend is freaked out at this point, as am I to say the least.

I stop immediately, but now we're both a bit scared from the children of the corn, and now this thing is literally within minutes of one another. We decide getting out is not going to happen, but I decide to stay in the locked car but use the car and its lights to see what we hit and make sure whatever the hell it was is dead. I needed to know what I just saw. I drive in tiny circles, backing up and forwards, looking for this creature but after checking every inch within 100 yards and not seeing anything including not a drop of blood where I hit it, straight on with a Benz. That was unnerving and although I wanted to check my mother's car, that would be dealt with further down the road. We were not going to get out there. So, we decided to head home at this point.

Fifteen minutes later I got back to the freeway, and I needed to get out and see how bad the car was. As I got out to check, quickly as I was not taking chances tonight, I noticed my grill was busted in but nothing too bad. I made sure it was secure and got back in as quickly as possible. My friend decided to stay inside the car.

Recently, I heard of the black-eyed kids and freaked out a little bit. I did not know that they were a real thing. I thought I just saw a couple of demon kids. I didn't know what to think. To this day, I've looked through tons of photos of supposed cryptid beasts and mythological creatures looking for what I hit. The closest I've found is some Algonquin drawings of wendigos and they were very close to what I believe I saw and hit that night. It seems to me very odd both things could happen so close to one another to not be related.

I would like to point out I've lived in Wisconsin a long time and it was not a deer or a coyote or anything else. What I hit was nothing native to the known Wisconsin landscape, and neither were those horrid kids. I will never forget either of those faces and just hope I never come across them ever again." HO

Both the black-eyed kids and the wendigo phenomenon are mentioned in this account. First, the black-eyed kids seem to be more of a supernatural scenario as opposed to a physical malady. Granted, the black eyes are very creepy. But I doubt that the black eyes remain in a permanent state. I have heard suggestions that these are "alien" or shapeshifting beings. There have also been descriptions of unnatural rapid movements or bilocation. If this is the case, then I would classify these as supernatural entities until proven otherwise.

The wendigo reference is also interesting since that term pops up occasionally when there is a discussion involving pale humanoids. A wendigo is defined as a mythological creature or evil spirit that originates from the folklore of First Nations based in and around eastern and central Canada and the United States. There have been instances of possessed humans who were said to resort to cannibalism once inflicted by an evil spirit.

In May 2020 I received an email from a Montana resident who was hearing horrible screams emanating from the mountains around their home:

"I lived in Montana on some land my dad owns. One day, I was hiking up a mountain, like most days. I heard this weird screaming coming from the other side of the mountain (away from my house and deeper into the woods). It wasn't a mountain lion because the scream was too deep and long (went on for about 10 seconds) and I'm pretty sure it wasn't a bear. It kind of sounded like a human, except it was distorted. It sounded like someone was possessed by something, sort of like what you'd hear in a horror movie.

I got to the top of the mountain, pulled out my binoculars, and looked in the general direction of the scream. I saw a weird humanoid-looking creature. It was as white as paper, didn't have any hair or clothes (or genitals), and its arms were longer than its body. It also had huge black eyes that covered most of its face. It was walking, but as soon as I saw it, it stopped and stared at me. I watched it carefully for at least 2 minutes. I remember thinking 'it's staring straight into my soul.' I had to look away because my eyes had started watering from not blinking.

When I looked back at it after wiping my eyes, it was gone. I couldn't see it anywhere, which made me think it was a weird hallucination or something. Illusion or not, I decided to get the hell away from the area and ran back home.

The scariest part is that 5 minutes after I walk in the door, I hear the scream again. It was much closer and made my ears ring. I'm pretty sure it was where I was standing when I first saw it. My dad heard it too, so it wasn't just some hallucination, and my neighbor was talking about the screams a week after it happened. I've researched it as best as I could, but never found anything fitting its description.

I've never seen it since. My dad hasn't either. It's one of the many reasons I moved in with my mom in Arizona." SH

In September 2011, the following narrative was forwarded by a friend who owns a security company. The witness is one of his employees who started working for him after serving several tours in Iraq and Afghanistan. He states that he worked for the US Army Criminal Investigations (CID) before and during the conflicts. He left the service for unspecified reasons. This account is secondhand, but I believe the witness' sincerity even though he wishes to remain anonymous. The anecdote was written by the witness and has not been edited except for some spelling:

"I was an investigator with CID from 2004–2009 and served in Iraq and Afghanistan. Most of my work was related to various schemes (bribery, money laundering, theft, etc.) by enlisted personnel.

In 2005 I was informed that I would be embedded with an Army infantry unit in a mountainous region in the Sulaymaniyah Governorate (northeast Iraq). Once I reached my assigned location, we were briefed on strange activity that had occurred in a particular area just a few miles from the Iranian border.

We started the investigation by reading reports that came from a few local villagers who stated that people were being hunted in the mountains by an unknown creature. One man told me that the Iranians called it a 'ghool.' He had never seen it, but it was described as a tall manlike creature with long arms and legs who fed on human flesh. I reported the information I gathered to my superiors after returning to the unit HQ.

A few days later I was ordered to return to the area of the strange activity and investigate further. An infantry squad with a squad leader was assigned to accompany me. The consensus was that it was likely a soldier who left his post (AWOL) and went batshit crazy and started causing problems. Armed conflict can induce the worst in people to surface. If this was the case and the individual was killing noncombatants, our job would be formidable.

After a few days of surveillance and searching, we had no clue what we were dealing with. If this was indeed a soldier or other civilian man, we would have seen him or gathered some evidence. I was starting to believe that this was a wild-goose chase, but the villagers insisted that there was something hunting them.

One evening the squad leader and I were going over a report when we were alarmed by a god-awful scream that came from the direction of a mountain pass that we had just searched a few hours before. A few local people who had been outside quickly made their way home. It was obvious that they had heard this scream before.

Within the hour the squad and I were slowly entering the

pass. It was night, but the moon was very bright, so we were able to see around a bit. We searched the entire area for several hours using night vision and high-intensity lights. We found nothing – not a footprint or remnant from any creature fitting the description.

I have always wondered what we heard that night. I have asked a few learned people for their opinion but with little satisfaction. There were many strange instances in Iraq that just never made the light of day. I heard of some, but I'm positive most were just filed away." NM

This is an interesting account. There have been humanoid claims by the Persians for almost nine hundred years. There is a Persian story about Ameen and the Ghool and the "Valley of the Angel of Death" as well as other folklore. I do hope that more of the strange phenomena experienced in Iraq and Afghanistan are disclosed at some point.

3

RAKES, FLESHGAITS, & OTHER MEMES?

At the beginning of the book, I explained the nexus of the memes and how certain monikers are used to identify the pale humanoids. Once again, the memes were identifiers of produced art and graphics that were distributed throughout the internet. As time went on, these memes were supposedly observed and encountered by witnesses as real corporeal beings. Thus, these witnesses referred to these humanoids as "Rakes," "Fleshgaits," "Crawlers," and a variety of lesser-known monikers.

The accounts that I will present are from actual witness statements and declarations. It is obvious that the witnesses, by their descriptions, thought that they encountered real flesh and blood entities. You, the reader, can interpret and determine the actuality of these humanoids. Is it possible that these beings could manifest as a thought-form by the human mind and be perceivable by the witnesses?

I received the following account in July 2014:

"I was walking late one night with my German shepherd when I smelled an overwhelming stench of roadkill. I looked over into the woods near my home and saw a naked pale white man-like thing crawling in the woods. It was on its hands, feet, and knees about three inches above the ground.

I changed hands with my flashlight which my dog's leash prevented me from immediately shining it in that direction. In the 2 seconds it took to change hands and shine the light on this thing, it had moved 20 feet to near a tree it was trying to hide behind. It saw my light as it was swinging towards it and quickly crunched into a cannonball-like posture and balanced on its toes & balls of its feet, hiding its face, and held perfectly still.

I got an overwhelming feeling that if I kept shining the light on it, that it would look up at me with glowing eyes and a weird face. So, I continued with my walk. I thought maybe it was a teenager doing a mime, but there was no one taking a picture and this thing had an oddly pronounced spine and was hairless.

I went home and looked on the internet to see if this is something kids are doing now (painting themselves white, shaving all hair off, rolling around in roadkill, and crawling around late at night in woods). Well, I found a picture on YouTube of a 'Rake' that a hunter's camera had taken that looked remarkably like this thing. I have no idea what it was, perhaps an underground dweller or ghoul – or God knows what. I live in a country suburb of Tampa, Florida, called Lithia. If you have any idea what this thing was, please let me know!" Name withheld.

The supposed hunter's trail camera image referred by the witness is generally known to have been a fake. The southwest region of Florida (the city of Tampa and the counties around it) is ripe with cryptid sightings and other unexplained activity, including UFOs.

I received a sighting report from CJ of the Laredo Paranormal Research Society in January 2016, who believes he encountered a "Rake" humanoid:

"My wife and I were returning from San Antonio, Texas, on a Sunday night sometime around May or June. My wife had fallen asleep and so I turned up the radio and drove south, taking I-35 into Laredo.

As we approached the north side of town, I turned the cruise control off and dropped down from 65 to 60 to negotiate the curve under the railroad bridge that crossed the interstate. I was in the right-hand lane as I came close to the bridge. That's when I spotted what at first looked like a homeless guy, completely naked, scuttling along the embankment of the road. He was skinny, pale-skinned, and his arms looked emaciated.

As I passed him, I had a creepy feeling that something about this person was all wrong. The way he moved as well as the way his arms and legs were more animalistic than human. With 26 years in law enforcement, I thought about stopping and going back to see what this guy was doing, however, with my wife along, and it was close to midnight, so I just kept going, figuring the guy was drunk. I told my wife about what I had seen when we arrived at our home. She thought it sounded like some drunken guy living under the bridge.

After meeting you folks and hearing about the show you do, I began listening when I have a chance. When you mentioned the Rake and described what people were reporting, I looked at the images on the internet. These images are reported to be of the Rake, and sure enough, that is what I saw. The creature was paralleling the road, so I never saw its face or eyes, but the body shape was as close to the drawings as I care to get.

Every time I approach that railroad bridge I slow down and take a second look, but so far I've only seen it the one time." CJ

Once again, the witness was positive that this was a real humanoid after comparing it to "Rake drawings" on the internet.

The following account was received in May 2017:

"Back in 2007 I and my ex lived in Cape Canaveral, FL. I was 23 at the time. One night (it was about 10 pm or 11 pm) I was talking to my friend on the phone and went outside to smoke. I was out there for a few minutes when I looked out at our Jeep. I saw this thing sitting on it. It was like a person but not a human. It was pale white and odd-shaped. It was crouching on the back of the Jeep. As I was looking at it, [it] slowly turned his head to look at me and its eyes are big and black. I immediately ran inside and told my friend I had to call her back later and I cried. My ex asked what happened. I tried to explain it but I couldn't find the proper words to explain the thing that I had seen.

For years I didn't know what to call this thing. I didn't know how to explain it and then I ran across [a] Rake drawing on the internet, and it looks exactly like the thing I saw. Years have gone by, and I've seldom thought about that thing, but recently gone back out towards Cape Canaveral it has been on my mind about every other day. It's terrifying. And at times it is very hard to sleep. When I close my eyes, I see it." TD

This witness thought that the "Rake" was a real being, expressing terror and consternation of the sighting still lingering in his memory.

I received this account in May 2017:

"Mr. Strickler,

"First off, I've been following your blog for a time, and I appreciate your steadfast work. I am an aspiring amateur paranormal investigator, and a big fan.

Now, let me start by saying that of the encounters I am about to describe, I have never personally experienced any of them, and this is due in part to the theory I will lay before you in good time.

I live in the western part of North Carolina, in the Blue Ridge Mountains near Asheville, and over the years have had several people visiting my neck of the woods describe rather frightening encounters with a similar phenomenon. The first note was years back, around 2008. A friend of mine and practicing medium met with me at Andrew's Geyser, a local monument known for its Civil War past and shadow people, and she claims to have seen a very disturbing creature, a gaunt humanoid with pale deathly flesh, willowy limbs, black eyes, and a gaping maw that seemed to emanate pure fear. She was very unsettled by this vision, but I never saw a thing. A few years later, 2011 or so, my significant other at the time would talk about a feeling of dread whenever she was alone in certain parts of the woods, and that she always had the feeling of being watched and unwelcome, occasionally seeing pale shapes dart in and out of the trees. Now, just in the past few days, around the 28th of April of this year, a close friend of mine was driving down a gravel road after visiting me and claims to have seen, crouching in the forest just off of the road up on a small rise, a pale and thin crouching figure. The description she gave was eerily comparable to the account given by my medium acquaintance years before, even eerier considering that these two have never met, yet describe the same entity. Their only connection is of course the woods, and I.

Now, in my college days I theorized with a friend what my medium ally had seen in 2008 and came up with an interesting hypothesis as to what she saw, what other people have encountered, and why I have never seen a thing, nor felt any unease or dread from these forests. The idea is thus: This creature, which bears many similarities to the Rake of quasi pop culture, is a Dryad gone bad. These forests have been periodically clear cut and burned by loggers and the railroad for decades upon decades at this point, and I believe that nature spirits or tree spirits who survive this will inevitably 'go bad' or turn feral. The reason I have never seen nor felt the dreadful presence of this entity is because I have lived and grown in these woods with the recovering forest since I was a child, and this Dryad sort of adopted and claimed me, which would, in turn, explain why certain women would experience a sense of unwelcome.

I therefore further theorize that these 'Rake' entities people seem to be experiencing are more of these Dryads gone feral and angry and will only be a more and more common encounter as industry and progress eat up more and more of their natural homelands.

Hope this information and ideas prove useful." JT

For the record, a Dryad is a supposed nymph or nature spirit who lives in trees and takes the form of a beautiful young woman. Dryads were originally the spirits of oak trees, but the name was later applied to all tree nymphs. I don't normally hear or read of these humanoids being compared to an entity from Greek mythology, but there does seem to be some local folklore involved with this.

In September 2018, I received an email and a telephone statement from a young female witness:

"My house has always been creepy. Growing up, I've had unexplained experiences starting from the time I was 4 and never stopping. I live in rural Kentucky. One of those towns that solely rely on coal and is 5 years behind the rest of the world. In general, the whole town is still covered in thick woods that appear to have not been tampered with in hundreds of years. My house is placed right in the middle of the mountains surrounded by a lot of woods and even a couple of ponds. That gives you the setting for my home.

This is where the real story begins. Growing up, I was never allowed to watch shows such as *Ghost Hunters* or even movies such as *The Exorcist* in my house because of the weird activity which goes on here. I'd experienced it from an extremely young age and my mom (who has lived in this house her whole life) had also. However, one night my family made an exception, and we all watched a documentary about Waverly Hills together. At that age, I still slept in the room with my mom due to me being afraid of sleeping in this house.

That night I woke up at 3 am to the feeling of something watching me. I felt extremely uneasy. I rolled over to look around the room and my eyes locked onto something standing beside my mom. It was extremely tall but looked as if it had a broken back and couldn't stand up completely. It was slouched over and had extremely pale skin and bones sticking out under the skin everywhere due to how skinny it was. It had long claws hanging from both hands. Its face was sunken in, and its eyes were completely black holes. A few greasy hairs were visible on its head. It had no clothes but also no genitals or nipples.

I was HORRIFIED. I rolled over and covered myself up to head to toe with the cover. I refused to move or look out the rest of the night even though I was fully awake. Eventually, my mom finally woke up that morning. She immediately started complaining of her side hurting. She raised her shirt to look and found huge claw marks down her side. It was three deep wounds that were extremely inflamed and still bleeding. I felt horrible knowing that thing did that to her while I lay beside her hidden.

A couple of months later I saw the creature again. Although, not as horrible as the first experience. I woke up to the creature slouched on the floor on my side of the bed. It was watching me sleep. I covered myself up again immediately, but this time got the courage to peek out and found it still looking at me. I'm not sure when it went away because I didn't dare look again. I got chills and my hair stood on end before even seeing it the first time. It had the feeling of complete evil to it.

I'm 18 now and sleep in my room. However, I still live in the same house. My mom still sleeps in the room where I witnessed this creature. Almost nightly she has nightmares about something watching her. She has nightmares about something hiding in the paintings on her walls or something coming from the ceiling in her room while she sleeps. There's one specific corner of the room where almost every dream seems to originate. Our cats refuse to stay in that room if the door is shut.

If anyone has any information about any folklore this could relate to, please tell me. I'm desperate for any information about what I've seen. Through my research, there is an entity call a 'Rake' that resembles what I saw. I've had countless other experiences in this house but those are the major ones." P

The witness told me that she had seen a drawing of a "Rake" and another graphic referred to as a "Fleshgait" online. She was sure that is what she and her mother had encountered. She insisted that this was not an apparition or ghost.

The following account was forwarded to me in April 2019 by a woman in the Florida Panhandle:

"I've been seeing this strange creature for the last 4 years, and it seems to follow me. As far as I know, the creature has never tried harming me, but it has oftentimes made me feel unsafe and threatened. As the years have passed, I've begun paying less mind to it and just putting the feeling in the back of my mind.

January 2012, I bought a horse and began boarding it at a very old barn. It was a small, tight-knit, friendly barn community not far from my home. It'd been around since the 60s, surrounded by woods. There were 3 barns, the main arena was surrounded by thick woods, and there were small trails in the woods behind the property.

Fast forward to June 2012, I had two horses there now. I was there every single day without fail, 2 pm–10 pm, I fed the horses and cared for them. I rode one every night as well, mainly in the arena, but sometimes in the barnyard. There were no field or arena lights, just the moon, and stars.

One evening, around 5 pm, I was sitting on her, letting her stand when she started snorting and backing up. I looked up and saw this white/grey creature crawling out of the woods towards us. It had a very small round head; its eyes were just pits. It had a very small mouth, not much detail there. Its arms were very long and thin, fingers also like that. Its rib cage was very pronounced and defined, and its legs were long and lanky. Its movements were very jerky, not smooth, and fluid. It slowly jerked out to us when my horse turned and bolted out of the arena. She's a dead broke, calm, well-mannered horse who never spooked before this. Stubborn old mare, but not spooky. She would not go back into the arena that night. I walked her around the barnyard, staying near the main barn, put her up, and ran out to peek into the arena, to find nothing except some 'footprints' where I saw the thing.

Throughout the summer, I saw it peeking, almost dancing, around the gate that led into the woods where the trails were.

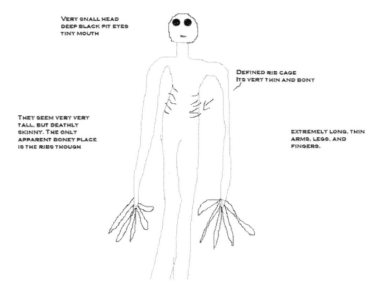

One night roughly a month later, at about 9 pm, I was riding that horse again in a front pasture. The moon was full and bright, and I looked to my left to see that creature running full spread by my side on the other side of the fence, I slowed my horse to a stop, and it took off around the corner and behind the side barn into the woods. I continued seeing it, mainly in the woods, but it was always around.

In summer 2013, the barn shut down when the owner died. We moved the horses to a friend's place for the time being, and I didn't see it there.

Early fall 2013, I found a new barn. Woods directly behind the barn and arena. This place had lights and was much newer. About a month later, when I was getting ready to leave, I heard something in the woods. I looked down the barn aisle into the woods and saw the creature running down the road into the woods. I saw it much less frequently for a while, until later in fall

2014 I began seeing it in the back of pastures woods, it darted in and out of the tree line.

I saw a second one sitting in a neighbor's yard. It would sit in the same spot every day and watch me ride.

I started taking pictures, which are very poor and crappy, and sent them to a friend who claimed he and some others have seen them.

Kept seeing it occasionally, but from a much greater distance than at the first barn. I went with this barn owner to another farm to get some stuff, when I saw a very large version of this creature run out from the woods, right behind a tree I was 10 feet from, while I was alone by the trailer.

Last November, I house-sat for the barn owners. I went out around 2 am to fill water troughs and enjoy the full moon and cool night. I was sitting in the back pasture when 3 of the creatures began coming from the woods, one came up to the trees near the trough where I was, the other two were walking along the tree line.

The horses were silently munching their hay, far from where the creatures were. I messaged the guy from earlier and told him what was going on. Since that incident, I haven't seen them.

Last summer, I did see one outside my house, staring into the windows. A few weeks ago, one was outside my bedroom windows, tapping and making a strange faint shrieking sound. My friend saw it and said that it was a 'Rake.' I have never heard that term before.

This was a lot to type out, but I hope someone reads this and helps me figure this out some more. I'm very open and willing to discuss more paranormal things that have happened with this, my friend's experiences with this, and anything else that could or could not be connected to this thing." KP

In some instances, these humanoids seem to follow people to other locations.

I received the following account in May 2019:

"One night two years ago, during the winter, I was leaving the house with a friend. As we were pulling out, we came to see a figure in the cornfield next to my house. As we got closer, we came to realize it looked human, but it wasn't. It had almost a petrified pale color and it was small, and on all fours, like the Gollum from *Lord of the Rings*, and it had pale eyes that looked hollow with dark spots around them.

We were both in my car and we didn't say anything as we saw it in my headlights. But as we passed it, we both asked each other if we had just seen that. I had completely forgotten about this story until recently when my friend brought it up to me.

I then asked my sister about it a few days later and she said I might have seen something called the Rake, so I looked it up. The thing looked just like how some of these pictures describe and I don't think I'll ever look at the paranormal the same ever again because of it." RF

In April 2020, the following incident descriptions were forwarded to me:

"I live in a very rural town in Mississippi where the majority of everything is forests or farms. My home happens to be very deep in the woodland area. It's almost like something out of a horror movie. The 'creepy old house in the middle of the woods'? Yep, that's my place.

Back when I first moved here, everything was normal. It was a quiet, peaceful house in the woods, the closest neighbors being 10 minutes or so down the road. Nothing out of the ordinary or weird. Until, one night.

I was driving home from work, it being nearly midnight, so it was almost pitch black. I was tired, ready to finally get home to sleep. I had let out a hearty yawn, closing my eyes for a split second, but that was all it took for me to almost hit something. Not even 10 feet in front of me sat this hairless man-dog-looking creature, the thing bloody and pale, hovering over the mutilated corpse of some animal. I hope it was an animal at the very least. The thing slowly looked up at me, staring me directly in the face with its beady, neon green eyes, shining due to my headlights reflecting off them. Its jaw looked almost unhinged, flaunting its many, many blood-covered teeth.

I was frozen with fear. WTF was that thing? I honked my horn, trying to scare it off, but it doesn't budge. It simply sat there. After what feels like a 30-minute staring contest, though it couldn't have been more than 2 minutes, the thing scurried away, walking on all fours. I watched it disappear into the thick mass of trees that matched the rest of the forest.

My eyes shifted back and forth from the forest to the carcass. I rubbed my hands over my eyes before continuing to drive. I still had a few minutes to my house, so I didn't worry about that thing appearing in my yard.

I haven't seen it plainly in front of me since (that was about 8 months ago) but I constantly feel as if I'm being watched or followed. I did my own research. Apparently, this thing is called the Rake? It's taken a liking to me, which scares me immensely. I'm constantly seeing it from a distance out of the corner of my eyes. Sometimes I see it for seconds at a time before it disappears into the woods again.

I know it watches me when I sleep. I had set up a camera, waiting for the unfortunate day where I wake up and see it. That'll be the day when it finally strikes." BC

The next incident report was received soon after:

"This happened in 2018 while my boyfriend at the time, myself and a friend were walking around near the river in our town. We live in a small town in Florida right on the St. Johns River. So, unless you're into fishing, there's not much to do.

It was getting late, around 10 pm when we decided to go check out this abandoned furniture factory a few streets over. When we got there, we checked the doors in the front to see if they were unlocked by any chance (they were locked of course). We walked to the side of it where it had been partially demolished a few years ago. The lower part of the walls that had been there was still standing, making a fence-like barrier we'd have to climb over. I leaned over the wall to see if we'd be able to walk through there, but there was too much rubble and weeds in the way. We decided to leave and head back to our cars.

I was halfway to the sidewalk when from the weed-filled

area came a deep growly 'Hey.' I stopped and looked behind me as I felt the color drain from my face. As I watched, I saw some of the weeds move. That's when I ran, leaving behind my boyfriend and friend. We ran almost two blocks before we stopped and started walking through the neighborhoods back to the cars. The entire way back, we heard something climbing across roofs, had rocks flung at us from the tops of trees, and a pale figure ran quickly past us. The entire time this was happening I had a strong feeling of dread.

We got back to our cars safely but stood there for a few minutes trying to calm down some before we drove. It was all calm for a minute before we heard the creature climb up onto the roof of a converted bank. It paced back and forth just out of the reach of the light, throwing things at us and into a tree a few times. It was so scary being followed like that through an area I used to feel so safe in.

I did some research when I got home and the growl, the paleness, and the speed at which it ran matches the description I found in Rake encounters. I think it only followed us and threw things because there were three of us there staying close together. Hopefully, I won't encounter it again, at least not alone." AS

The previous two accounts were interesting because it seemed as if the entities were stalking the witnesses. It is a reoccurring theme in many of these encounters, though it isn't always apparent that the witnesses are being stalked or if the entity is exhibiting curiosity.

The next incident in north-central Alabama was received in April 2020:

"Two of my friends (who are a married couple) and I were walking on my family land. It's about 170 acres and heavily wooded with both pines and hardwoods, and heavily trailed. It was dark but my friends wanted me to take them out walking on the trails. A couple of the neighbor's dogs followed us (a Coonhound and Great Pyrenees), and we walked south then east to my camping area.

We were hanging out at my camping spot when behind us, further back the trail we had come down, the dogs started acting strange. We were looking back, and they came out of the woods to our left and stood on the trail. The Great Pyrenees started growling and looking defensive. The Coonhound is a goofball, but he was also acting disturbed about something. They were both looking back down the trail to the west. I immediately got quite a strange and serious feeling. It was a bit ominous. I've learned to trust my gut, which I recommend to anybody in the woods, or if around a person or animal that you feel instinctively is threatening.

Anyway, I told my friends that we had better get back to the house 'now.' Well, we were heading west on the trail, and the dogs, if I remember correctly, had vacated the area. While walking, I looked back and saw my one friend, the wife, looking into the woods off the trail and stagger back a few steps. Her husband had walked ahead, and I asked her what was wrong. (By the way, this is the area where the dogs had previously been growling at.) She said to me, 'I'll tell you when we get back, I don't want to scare him (her husband).' He's kind of easily spooked.

So, we get back and I asked what she saw. She tells us that she felt she needed to look off the trail, into the trees, and she saw something halfway behind a tree, looking at her (we all had headlamps on). She said it was human-like, pale, whiteish, with an oval kind of shaped head. Looked like it was crouching, with long limbs. She kept stressing how skinny it was, particularly the limbs. She said it had a surprised look on its face like it didn't expect us to be there. My friends, relatives and I use the trails regularly, but not at night. She said that the thing was bobbing back and forth in kind of a creepy way. It moved its head behind the tree and then was swaying its head and shoulders back rhythmically to look at her. She said it didn't appear to be aggressive but looked scary. I pulled up the famous trail cam pic of the 'Rake,' or whatever it is, and she got a shocked look on her face and nodded. However, she made it clear that it wasn't the same.

The next night, I was on the back porch and heard a freaky, very shrill scream coming from the woods. I don't know if the two were related, but I've lived in the country for most of my life, and I've never heard anything like it. This is one of many things that have happened around here, but this is the only one that I know of involving this creature. This is in north-central Alabama." KB

I was receiving a constant stream of reports from witnesses during the spring of 2020. I don't know if it was because of the Covid epidemic, and people were coming forward with past experiences while at home or not:

"I work as a paramedic in a rural area of Virginia. This entails a lot of backwoods and mountain roads late at night. This encounter happened around the summer of 2016.

One night around 2 am or 3 am I was driving back from a call and was traveling up a road I have been up many times before. My partner and I were just listening to music and making the best of being at work. As I rounded an upwards slanted curve, the headlight of my unit hit something that still gives me chills as I'm typing. This creature was almost in a position that reminded me of a catcher in baseball as if it was squatting beside the road maybe ten feet in a small grassy patch. It was so pale and white. I distinctly remember its arms and legs being so long. Just unnaturally long and slender, and its fingers were the same. If I had to estimate the height, I would say it was easily 6 feet tall. Its head was facing away from me. I honestly did not get a good look to see any facial features. I was shocked. I didn't speak a word. I turned to my partner who was in the passenger seat, and the look on his face told me I was not seeing an imaginary thing. I said to him to please tell me you saw that. He did, with a variety of colorful words.

It may have been 50 yards away when we agreed to turn around and look again. When we got back to the same place there was nothing. I didn't dare get out of the ambulance to check. My partner did pull out a spotlight we have in our units to check the woods and again nothing. I can't stress enough how pale, boney and slender this creature was. It was like the Pale Man from 'Pan's Labyrinth' but I could see every bone in its body. I only got a two to three-second look at this creature." KK

The witness didn't describe it as a Rake until I talked to him.

Here's another witness account that came to me around the same time:

"I am still at a loss for words to explain how scary this is, most [of] all because it is no doubt something NOT human or any known animal. This is taking place nightly behind a close friend's home not far away and started last fall. The area is in north Florida (near Wakulla) in a very rural area, and behind her house is wild bamboo that has completely overgrown the land surrounding the ruins of an old house that literally collapsed or imploded somewhere approximately 15 years ago. These things have not only taken over back there but have been seen by several of us, but never in the daylight. This started with a mound appearing that wasn't there before last fall that was large and built entirely of heavy debris from that house and broken bamboo. This is scary considering no person can break the bamboo.

Since it first appeared, this mound has constantly expanded in width and height to an alarming size and has cave-like openings in it. Now they have dug large and long tunnels going underneath it.

Now I'm concerned as one of them has been seen coming out of the bamboo and underneath her house, under the addition in the back where her dogs will not go alone and act purely terrified, even though still inside the house. We now know that's because these dogs have known this thing or more than one has been under her kitchen floor nightly for who knows how long. The land around the old house has a very strong and bothersome vibe to it.

What we have seen is a very thin and pale figure which doesn't appear to have normal legs and is very elusive. Aside from very sinister-looking yellow glowing eyes, I haven't seen or has anyone else seen any other facial features. What do we do? Is this a Rake? I want to get documentation of this, which I do have pics of this structure they built over time. But none of us will dare attempt to even go out her back door at night at the edge of the bamboo." U

The next account was forwarded around the same time:

"I live in Wyoming, Michigan, walking distance away from the Resurrection Cemetery. The tree line closest to the woods is where I've seen the Rake each time. I have multiple stories, but I'll try to share only the most unusual incidents.

The first encounter I had was with my sister while she was going to take a walk through the cemetery. It was late at night, and I had the gut instinct to go with her, so I did. We decided to play *Pokemon Go*. I didn't like the forested area around it, especially this big pine tree visible by a maintenance path that led to the crematorium. I was scared out of my mind, but we went towards the crematorium anyway to get a Pokestop and a Jigglypuff. We had to go so close that we were on the maintenance path, but the nicer cobblestone half. It was when I looked to my right that I first saw it, hunched over. It looked like a normal human being but more terrifying. It appeared to have seen me too because it stood up. I could tell it was tall, I'd estimate about 7 feet in height. I told my sister to run, and we ran home where I proceeded to pray in my room for a while.

My mom had a sighting as well. She had mentioned seeing something grey hunched in the top of the pine tree I mentioned earlier, and it was watching us. When she looked back it was gone. Safe to say, we went home early that day. My mom described the creature and I recognized it as something I'd drawn a few weeks before.

My most recent sighting (and the one that kept me from going back to the cemetery) happened in broad daylight with a friend. I'll keep his name hidden for privacy, but we decided to go to the cemetery after class (college program but for high school freshmen). We wandered around the cemetery for hours, until my arm started hurting and I decided that we should go home for a snack. As we walked my anxiety heightened. I had told him about the Rake, but I suspected we wouldn't have to worry as it was daytime.

As we were walking along the sidewalk, about to reach

the tree line, I saw a dead squirrel and a dog leg in the middle of the sidewalk. I looked up and I saw the Rake run straight into the tree line. It was gray and ran on all fours rather than on two legs. I told my friend to run. We both ran until we reached the intersection." M

References to the "Rake" by British witnesses is not common, though more recently, there have been more accounts surfacing. That's the case with the following report I received in June 2020:

"As a teen, I just refused to sleep at normal hours, especially on weekends. Why? Well, that's because the house I lived in and the land the house was on was haunted. Staying up usually meant seeing some freaky activity and growing up in a small English town in Berkshire, well, that's as exciting as life got.

So, one night when I was around 14, I was staying up staring out my window when I started seeing glowing blue and purple lights coming from the forest behind my house (we don't have fireflies where I lived). I thought they were cool, so I just continued staring at them, trying to figure out what they were. Now the way my house was set up, my bedroom window faced the forest and my back garden, and directly next to my room is a side gate that links to the front part of the house. On either side of the gates are motion sensor lights.

So, the lights in the forest may not have been paranormal but what happened next most definitely was. The motion at the front of the gate triggers, casting a faint light into my garden. The night grows silent, no more owls or crickets and just eerie. The lights in the forest seem to ebb and then just die out. I listen carefully as I start to hear scuttling on the wood of the gate. It's muffled so I slightly crack open my window to get a better look and listen.

Now that gate is always locked, with a heavy padlock at that. To this day I have asked my dad if he ever left the gate unlocked that night, and he stands by the fact that unless he's gardening, the gate stays closed. This was spring so he might have started seeding so for my comfort of mind, I'm going to assume he left the gate open.

Anyways, I hear the gate slowly swing open. The creaks of the wood were so loud against the silent night, so the sound was very distinctive. The motion light right underneath my bedroom window switches on. Honestly to this day I really can't explain what I saw.

It was this off-white veiny kind of skin texture and was about the size of a child. It walked on all fours and looked just sickly. Its hind legs were significantly longer than its front legs and it looked to have hand claws? I hate having to link back to creepy pasta but it honestly looked like the Rake.

Now I've gone through the possibilities in my head. It was too small to be the deer that frequented our garden, also it had no remotely deer-like features. A badger or fox with a disease is possible. However, I've never seen badgers or foxes with such long limbs and so disproportionate. Also, this thing was completely hairless and humanlike.

The worst part about it to me was how it slowly and silently moved up my garden path before disappearing into the woods. The noises of the night started back up after that, but I was frightened, and I didn't sleep that entire night.

I'm from England so I haven't heard of any folklore that matches what I saw. I know there were occult practices done in the woods behind my house but I'm pretty sure it was pagan, hence not inherently bad or demonic.

I don't know what I saw." LB

The following account is a bit unusual. A Canadian woman says that she only witnessed a humanoid, which she referred to as a Rake, when in the presence of her Swedish ex-boyfriend. Since then, the same entity has again manifested around the ex-boyfriend and his new girlfriend. I received the account in June 2020:

"In 2012, my (then) boyfriend lived in Sweden. I live in Canada. He came to visit me and, during one of the evenings, I woke up to something strange perched at the foot of the bed. It was a pale, thin humanoid figure. It was completely hairless, and the legs seemed to be bowed in some way. It seemed to walk on all fours despite looking human. I couldn't see much of its face since it was looking away from me. It looked a lot like the creature from the fictional story 'The Rake.' When I gasped, it hopped off the bed and into the darkness. My partner heard me and woke to ask me what was wrong. I didn't tell him as to not cause alarm while he was trying to rest.

In 2014, he was visiting once more, and we were once again in bed sleeping. I woke up to hear my boyfriend screaming as I've never heard before. I immediately turned on the light and shook him to try to snap him out of it but he just screamed and then cried. After 30 or so minutes he finally was calm enough to explain what happened. Apparently, he woke up to a pale, humanoid figure with a gaping mouth and black, sunken eyes basically on top of him. As he screamed the figure slowly backed itself into the closet hole, staring at him, crawling on all fours. I felt sick. I never ever told him about what I saw a few years prior. There's no way he could've known and described what I saw perfectly like that.

Now it's shown up again. My ex messaged me today

(we're friends) and told me his current girlfriend has seen the pale 'man.' They were asleep and apparently, she woke up to see this thing stalking around the room and it noticed her frozen in fear, so it crawled up next to her. My ex woke up and tried to console her. She described what she saw, it apparently was a perfect exact match to the thing we both saw. I only ever told him what I saw after his experience, and she has never heard of either of our experiences.

Is this just a mass coincidence of hallucinating while waking up? Is it a demon or some sort of haunting? I'm really freaked out." SH

I supposed the question should be asked. Can crawler humanoids and, for that matter, meme humanoids manifest due to other paranormal activity or energy being present? We have long suspected that cryptids, like Bigfoot, may be related to other aspects of the paranormal, namely UFOs, extraterrestrial and spirit energy. But is it possible that a thought-form or tulpa may also be created separately from the subconscious mind?

The remaining chapters will include accounts and reports of undetermined humanoids of various descriptions, from other worldwide locations, and beings that exhibit opposing mannerisms. What are they? Is it possible that a new humanlike species is developing in our midst?

4

THE HUMANOIDS...AND EVERYTHING IN BETWEEN

Since 2013, there has been an explosion of pale gangly and emaciated humanoid reports surfacing worldwide. But most of these incidents are occurring in North America, particularly in the United States. The following accounts represent an accurate representation of what everyday people are experiencing.

―――――

UNITED STATES

IN AUGUST 2017, I RECEIVED A REPORT FROM PIERCE County, Missouri, that centered around a Gollum-like being that was seen feeding on a dead horse that it had killed:

> "I lived in a small town in Missouri called Pierce City. I had saved up a good 4 years' worth of paychecks and sold my TV to buy a used Suzuki SV650. It was my dream bike. I went and bought it and my father helped me get it to our home because I wasn't legally able to ride it for another few weeks. I

remember when we got home, I put it in our barn and locked the barn because we didn't have a garage. I don't remember why I did it though it's a very small town and we knew pretty much everyone and are hours away from the nearest neighbor.

I fell asleep about 10 pm or 11 pm and woke up at 3 am because I heard a large bang near the barn. I thought it was one of the horses that might have got spooked or something, so I went out to check. I always carry a Buck 110 folding blade and when I got to the barn it was still locked. There are no windows, besides one way at the top, but it's a good 15ft high and there wasn't a ladder. I unlocked the barn and walked in, and my new (used) bike was on the floor. I heard a crunching/chewing noise, so instinctively I grabbed my knife. There was very little light just enough to reflect the polished metal.

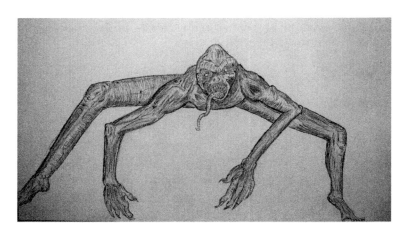

I peeked into the pen, and I kid you not, there was something squatted over the horse who it had to have killed as it was a healthy animal, and we took good care of it. I've seen wolves eat animals before and it wasn't like that it looked like the thing from *The Lord of the Rings*, the cave dweller thing but taller, and I know it was only a couple of seconds, but it felt like minutes of me being frozen there. Whatever it was looked at me and I turned and sprinted back to the house screaming. I swear it chased me. It ran on all fours and screeched like worn brakes on a heavy vehicle. I must have awoken my dad as he met me at the door with his gun loaded and fired two shots in its direction and then shoved me inside and shut the door. It seemed scared of the shots, and we later dialed the police, though they found nothing. If you guys live near there and have heard anything of it, please tell me. It still haunts me, and I live nowhere near there now." G

The next account was a follow-up to a MUFON report from May 2014, which was investigated by a colleague in Lubbock, Texas. It is an excellent example of how the presence of these humanoids can cause a disruption in the witness' mental well-being:

"I was sitting in a dark room looking out into the kitchen area. It was early morning. I suddenly saw something very tall and white move across the kitchen almost in a stroll, like it owned the house. It went past the door, so I didn't get a good look, but I knew automatically it wasn't human. I froze, scared to death. My husband and my young daughter were in the living room just about 10 steps behind this creature. Not only that I couldn't hear it moving around. The creature was a little over 6 feet tall. My first thought when it went by was to make myself believe it was my husband walking over to the kitchen area. But when I finally got my nerve to get up and walk, I realized I was right, and it was not my husband.

You could almost feel that it knew the house and us more than anything, which is very disturbing. The creature didn't seem to have an ounce of fat on its body, but very strong looking with muscles, but quite thin. Its body looked like it was covered by some sort of bodysuit that looked like pale skin.

I'm scared to death. I can't tell you how for the first two months I screamed in the car and cried. I had a feeling that if this thing wanted to kill us, there's nothing that we can do to stop it. No weapon would be effective against it. I felt we were cattle to be harvested for food and, as a mother, I had a horrible sense of hopelessness. I've never in my life had such hopelessness. There's no place to go, no place to hide. There's nothing you can do. I hate the feeling.

I have not told anyone, not even my husband. I can't. I feel if I utter the words out loud, whomever I tell the story [to] will die.

I wake up, as I always do, around 3:30 am and I think I hear something. Still worried about being slaughtered, I stayed still and glanced around the room. I didn't want anything to know I was awake yet. I could feel myself sweat and I had to tell myself to take slow steady breaths to make it look like I was still asleep.

I suddenly heard something sliding against the ceiling of the room. I remember my heart was pounding and I could still hear the steady breathing of my husband sleeping next to me. The ceiling fan was going, and I had the covers pulled up around me. The sliding was approaching me. Then suddenly I caught sight of a pale being sliding across the ceiling with its head hanging down. I watched it as it slid around the room and slowly above me. I closed my eyes, laughing at myself thinking I'm so silly and I'm just being paranoid.

I eventually went into a depression. I didn't know what life was anymore. I couldn't tell anyone anything verbally without giving them some type of death wish. But then, one day, I'm fine. It's strange. I don't mind if the creature is here or not. I feel like I should protect it. I feel like if it wants to communicate it can. But I still feel if I utter a word verbally and if it finds out, that person will die." Name withheld.

Occasionally, these intense encounters may result in paranoia. But that is usually an exception to the norm. Most incidents are fleeting, and the being moves on to another location. It's rare for one of these humanoids to stay for an extended period. But it does happen.

The late UFO/paranormal investigator and my friend Chris Holly told me about a strange account that was forwarded to her.

Chris mentioned that she received an email from a woman who lived on the end of Long Island, New York, at Montauk Point. She told me that she often walked her two large dogs on the beach along the Atlantic Ocean coast at the point. The woman told Chris that she often reads her articles and remembered one that she wrote years ago about a strange, tall, very white, odd-looking family who lived on Long Island in the 1960s.

This lady told Chris that while walking her two large dogs during December and January, she witnessed a strange family with a huge, strange dog also walking on the beach. She told her that they were extremely tall and seemed to be an albino couple with about four or five children with them running along the beach. She told Chris that she remembered her article and wanted to know if she had any other reports of this strange family being seen on Long Island.

Chris told me that she contacted the woman, who told her that she had stopped seeing the strange family at the end of February. She told Chris that she found them to be so very odd that she asked her friends and neighbors if they had seen the family. The only other person who claimed to have seen them was an older man who would feed the birds along the shore on the beach, but he only noticed them once and did not recall ever seeing them again.

Chris questioned her and found the woman to be concerned about the people, as she felt they were something other than human and felt very uncomfortable when walking near them. She told Chris her large dogs, who were very protective and a bit on the aggressive side, would whimper and stick their tales between their legs, dragging her away from the family.

Chris then forwarded me an article that she wrote about these strange tall white people and was wondering if they are being seen anywhere else in the world. Chris told me that if they are being seen, then who are they and where did they come from?

Here is the article she forwarded to me, with full permission to use:

"Years ago, I was sitting on my deck with my mother having lunch when my mother looked over to me and said, 'Remember the albino family that used to live in our area that always shopped at Gertz Department store?'

I hadn't thought about Gertz Department store, which had long ago gone out of business, for years, much less the albino family.

My mother went on about how striking they were and how well dressed and groomed they were. My mother had commented many times how beautiful the family was and that she always noticed what they were wearing. I never thought much about it then, as I was in my teens, but as my mother went on and on about the albino family, I realized how very strange they were.

The family consisted of two adults and three children.

All of them were albinos. I have only seen a few other people who have this albino condition and did not note the differences in this family and the other albinos I have seen. Talking to my mother about this family, I began to realize they were truly unusual people and not like other albinos.

The five members of this family all were 6 feet in height, including the mother and daughter. The male members stood between 6 feet 3 inches to 6 feet 5 inches. They were extremely tall people. When they walked through the department store, they stood a head above most of the other shoppers.

Each of them had thick full pure white hair. They were beautiful people with high cheekbones and straight model-like features. Their skin was white, immaculate alabaster white. They all had the same color eyes, which were clear, big, and very light blue. They kept to themselves. They would stay together when they shopped and seemed to be quiet and polite people.

It wasn't until years later and I had that conversation with my mother about that family that I realized they were a very different group of people. I thought about the possibility of two beautiful albino people who looked so much alike in height, looks, and facial features meeting and marrying. Although this is possible, I knew the odds had to be nearly impossible. I then recalled reading an article while in college in the late 1970s that talked about all the eye problems that went hand and hand with those who were albinos. I also read that eye color for the typical albino runs towards the pinkish reddish tint. I know that there are degrees of the condition which would have a lesser or greater effect on things like eye and skin color (or lack of it) in those who are albinos. I did not read about any who had clear big blue eyes.

I tried to find out if there were blue-eyed albinos that

could run in an entire family but came up empty-handed in my search. I am not qualified to answer the question to the chance of this happening but feel at best it would be a very rare occurrence.

I thought about this family and had to admit that finding two tall beautiful blue-eyed albinos who married and had three tall beautiful blue-eyed children was either an incredible happening or they were not a family of albinos!

Years after discussing this family with my mother, I came across a few articles on the internet that talked about the tall whites. I was scrolling down one of the pages of the site I was looking at when I came to an artist's drawing of the alien species called the 'Tall Whites.' I was completely taken aback as I sat and looked at the same tall people with the same beautiful faces – white hair, blue eyes, and high cheekbones as the albino family on Long Island.

I will never know if that strange gentle family of tall, beautiful people was simply a very rare family of human albinos or if they were a group of entirely different beings?

I often wondered over the past years about that family or group of people. I have tried to search for them a few times but cannot find anything anywhere that would explain this odd group of people. Maybe they just moved away to another state – or planet!

I did learn to not be so ambivalent about things and pay attention to people and my surroundings far more than I once did. I wish I had been more curious at the time. I wish I considered how odd those people were and thought about things instead of just blindly skipping along without considering what was going on around me."

The account is different than the pale humanoids that this book is covering. But it does make you realize that oddities are present throughout our world, and that we simply don't have an explanation for everything.

I received this disturbing account in July 2015:

"I'm a truck driver and I was heading east on I-80 up through to Illinois. I had stayed the night, well, the afternoon in Des Moines, Iowa, to get some sleep. I got a fresh eight hours of sleep and I had just got on the road.

It was about dusk, and the sun was just about to set. I was driving and I saw a figure just ahead of me on I-80 and it was right on the side of the road. When I say right on the side of the road, I don't mean in the grass. Its toes were right on the white line. I slowed down a little bit to kind of see what was going on there and maybe avoid it. I got about fifty yards from it and slowed to 50 miles per hour. I could see it clearly since I had my high beams on.

It was a man. Well, it looked like a man about maybe 5'9" or 5'10". He couldn't have been more than a hundred pounds soaking wet. And when I got up to him, he looked at me and, I kid you not, he had no eyes, no mouth, no nostrils. There was no orifice on his face. He was pale white. No hair. No features whatsoever. It looked like a skeleton with bleached white skin. He was just kind of standing there looking right at me. I slowed down and as soon as I saw his face, he looked up at me, boy, I flipped the hammer down the entire way to Chicago. I never looked back. My blood ran cold. My hair stood up. It was one of the most disturbing things I've ever seen in my life." BB

I received the following bizarre report in December 2016 from a resident of Pennsylvania:

"In 1999 I was working at a state park in Centre County, Pennsylvania, and got to know the back areas of it pretty well. Approximately one mile from the park on a long all-dirt road was a large clearing in the woods which was cleared for power-lines and gas well use. Once you got to that spot you would have to walk over a long hill until you came to an old, abandoned trail. If you followed this trail, it would take you deep into the forest.

One day I followed it and found that it led to a dilapidated cabin (not on the park cabin records) and it looked like it hadn't been used for many decades. Even though it was daylight I still got this creepy feeling like I shouldn't be there and worse that something was watching every move I made.

A few weeks later, while I was off-duty, two of my friends and I were just out driving around enjoying the summer night and, since I knew all the back roads, I was taking them on kind of a tour (none of these roads are off-limits or secret so I wasn't breaking any rules). Other than that mysterious cabin the park hasn't any secrets. About 11:00 pm I came to that familiar clearing, and I mentioned something about the old cabin. Being a brave soul, I talked them into letting me show them the cabin, so I grabbed my flashlight, and we took off down the hill and onto the path that led to the cabin.

I took the lead and we walked halfway when my light flashed on something on the right side of the path. Almost immediately I stopped and said, 'Did you just see that?' To which they responded, 'See what?' As I panned the light back to the right side of the road I said, 'THAT!' There standing by a tree was a creature only seen in sci-fi movies. It had a greyish olive skin with thin extremities. The calves and forearm muscles were very large as well as the chest. The face was the strangest thing since it had an oval head but there was no mouth. It had a nose that was long and thin but not longer than its chin. The eyes had a reddish hue in the light and were very small. I hate to make this reference for fear of questioning my sanity, but my best description was like what the 'Goons' looked like in the Popeye cartoon. It was leaning oddly against the tree.

Immediately everyone wanted to leave, but as we turned, my flashlight went out. My friends told me to quit messing with them and turn the light back on to which I informed them that I wasn't messing with them and to keep moving now that I was at the back of the group. I frantically continued to beat on my flashlight trying to get it to work again. As soon as it came back on I immediately swiveled back around to shine it behind us. The creature had moved up significantly and now was on the left side. We hurried to the clearing and once we got back up the hill and to the main dirt road things got worse. Out of [the] woods we had just come through was this high-pitched blood-curdling screeching noise which, after it started, others started to 'answer' back from the other side of the clearing.

The fact that I was a park ranger, who had been in the woods all my life and had my degree from Penn State in wildlife management, means I've heard a lot of noises in the wild. But I have never heard that sound before. I know it wasn't any kind of owl or bobcat, bear, bird, porcupine, etc.

Several months went by without incident, other than not being able to shake that, 'I'm watching you' feeling. I was to the point of feeling like I was being stalked.

One night I went to get something from my truck when I looked into the woods and saw those reddish glowing eyes staring at me in the shadows. I immediately ran into the house and grabbed my biggest knife (I'm not a gun guy) to which my father asked me what I was doing. I told him I was tired of feeling 'stalked' and was going to face this thing. He told me he was coming with me (but all along I knew he never truly believed me or my encounter). When we got outside, he nonchalantly asked, 'Ok, where did you see this thing?' I pointed to the spot to which he directed his flashlight. Much to his disbelief there it was, and as soon as the light hit it, [it] tore off deep into the woods. My father, an ex-Marine who served proudly during Vietnam, yelled at me to get back into the house with fear. There was real FEAR in his voice.

To this day it still creeps me out telling this encounter and my hands shake even while typing while recalling it all. I am now in my 30s with a wife and kids, but even now, when I go outside at night, I still feel watched to the point that when I get a real strong feeling my wife won't let me leave the house without her.

Just as a side note, for the first 5 years of our relationship she too would catch sight of this creature, but mostly as it was going into the shadows. Thank you for your time." Ben

For most of 2016, then into 2017, I had been investigating sightings of an unknown humanoid in and around the Big Bear Lake, California, area. This also included areas southeast into Big Morongo Canyon and along Route 62 into Yucca Valley and Joshua Tree.

There had also been reports of people going missing in the area for several years, and a few body parts were recovered by police. In fact, there had also been sightings of a winged humanoid in Yucca Valley.

That being stated, in November 2017, I received the following account:

"On the night of February 27, 2017, in the early morning, I was staying at the Best Western in Big Bear, California. At

approximately 12:35 am I walked to my car alone to retrieve
my luggage. It had been snowing and was extremely dark, my
car was facing a country road. When I hit the unlock button
on my car, the parking and interior lights came on. This
allowed me to see two eyes reflecting in the middle of the
road, about 10-15 ft from me. At first, I thought it was a deer,
I have lived in Colorado, and I'm accustomed to seeing
wildlife.

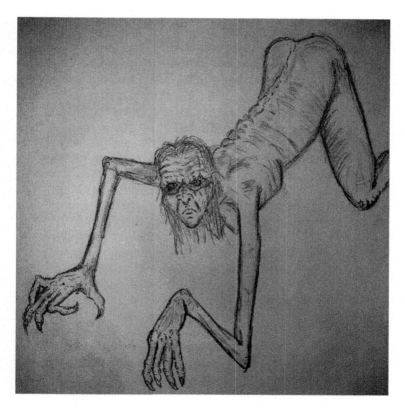

I instantly stopped and remained still as I didn't want to scare
off what I thought was a deer. As my eyes glanced down-
wards, I noticed it wasn't a deer. It looked like a white, hair-

less naked man on all fours. It was at least four feet in height, on all fours. There was a brief instance when our eyes made contact. It then, as quickly as I have ever seen any animal, turned around, ran as fast as a cheetah away from me, then, straight up a tree. I was frozen in disbelief. Just as I was going to convince myself that this couldn't possibly be happening, it leaped from treetop to treetop.

I've never heard of such a creature, but I have found some other videos and pictures online that look exactly like what I saw.

The speed and strength were like nothing I've ever heard of before. The creature was solid. It then appeared as if it was coming toward me, possibly hunting me? I don't know what stopped it. Was it the lights that went on? It had no visible genitalia. It had human-like qualities.

If this had been a huge-eyed gray alien, it would have made more sense. I've heard of those, but this was unlike anything I've ever been familiar with.

None of this makes sense to me, the speed, agility of the creature, and there shouldn't be any way that the treetops should have been able to hold the weight of the creature. It appeared to be flashing like a TV going in and out of reception as it sprinted up the tree. It also didn't appear to disrupt the foliage as it did so.

I immediately called my father after I rushed back into my hotel room. My son was asleep, and I was understandably in a state of shock. At this time, no one knew what hotel I was staying in. As I was crying on the phone to my father, the hotel phone rang. I answered it and it was only a dial tone. Then, there was a knock at the hotel room door. Once again, no one was there.

At this point, my son woke up due to the commotion. I told him it was a scary dream. I gave my father the hotel information and he advised me to go wait in the lobby with my son. As we were leaving, there was another knock, but it was at the back sliding glass door that went out to a privately fenced-in patio.

This was a one-time encounter and it's unfortunate that I still live in fear of this experience. I was raised as a Christian. This humanoid doesn't fit into any category with which I am familiar. I don't know why this happened and what I'm supposed to learn from it.

My previous beliefs on the world and the way things work have been tossed upside down. While it's thought-provoking, it's been very traumatic and has me in a panicked state that's distracting and mostly negative." N

I never did resolve the humanoid sightings in the area. The witness was very disturbed by the encounter, even after talking to her about the incident a year later.

I received the following account in December 2017:

"I live in Fulton County, Illinois, near Pekin. This is a legit sighting I had on October 25, 2017. We were walking through a trail in the woods at around 10 pm. While walking through we heard a weird screeching sound, almost like a tree squeaking which is what we thought it was, but it was everywhere we went in the woods it was squeaking.

When we came back into the woods on the same trail 'it' was there on the side crouched down facing and staring at us. It wasn't making the noise that we heard earlier though. I think it was about 5 feet tall if standing, but that's a prediction. It crouched down and was probably around 3 and a half feet in height in that position. It was light gray, and it didn't seem to have any hair or fur. The arms were very human-like with 5-fingered hands, but the legs looked webbed like a frog.

The eyes were small and dark. The head wasn't very large compared to the body. It was around the same body proportions as a human. But the head shape was different than a human head shape. The head shape was more square-like but rounded. I couldn't tell if they were ears or something else. The torso was covered up by the arms and legs so I can't explain it. The arms were very defined and slightly muscular. It tilted its head and stared at us, almost like it was alarmed or frozen.

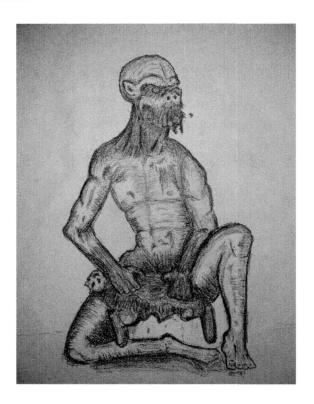

We turned our backs and ran because we were shocked and fearful. I've been researching for almost 2 months but have little idea of what we encountered." P

This next account was received in April 2018:

"Lon, this is a close encounter with an otherworldly being. This is not a hoax, and I don't care if it's not believable because I still try to convince myself to this day that it was only a dream, but I can't.

Me and a friend were driving home during the early morning hours in 2009 here in south Texas, near Brownsville. A bipedal, hairless, and pale glowing humanoid jumped out of the brush towards my car as we passed. We were driving at 20–25 mph. This being screamed at us with a very shrill high-pitched yell. I'll never forget it.

When I fully looked at this humanoid my heart just stopped. It did not look anything like a Hollywood character of what an alien might look like. It was not of this world.

We then sped off as fast as we could and did not look back. I just wanted to get it off my chest." NV

I then received this report in June 2018 from Superior, Wisconsin:

"My cousin and I had just finished eating dinner after playing a round of golf. We were driving on a two-lane road that leads back into the east side of our city. As we turned right at a corner that leads back onto the main road, we drove another 100 feet until on the right side of the road I saw an 8-foot-tall figure that was walking back into the edge of the forest located under a street light. I immediately hit the brakes, unsure of what I saw. My cousin who was in the passenger seat looked as shocked as I was. I yelled, 'I think that was an alien.' The car came to a stop and my cousin yelled, 'Go, go, go!' I sped up and my eyes were tearing up as I couldn't believe what I had just seen. My cousin said, 'I thought I was seeing things!' I replied with, 'No, I saw it too!'

We drove to our apartment, which is nearby, still shocked and startled. I immediately called some friends. They came and picked me up and drove us back to the spot where I saw the figure. I explained what happened to them, and when we drove back to the location some brush had looked to be parted where something large had walked through it. I made the call to the hotline next where a gentleman told me to make this report and call local authorities which are being called now.

The figure stood 8-9 feet tall, had a tall-rounded crown shape head. The head was as big as a human abdomen, the figure was somewhat muscular looking. It had big eyes, but not stereotypical alien-like, long legs, and it did not seem startled whatsoever. It was pale green all over. What was that thing?" D

The following odd account was received in May 2018:

"I was looking for a spot to set up a quick campsite in a small patch of woods along a public bicycle path in west central Ohio. I was cold and eager to get a small fire going and get inside my sleeping bag. The area is a refuge for stray cats. Many locals drop off their unwanted or stray cats in this area and some local kind-hearted folks feed them and provide plastic containers for shelter. When I found what I thought would be a suitable spot to set up camp, I laid my bag down and walked a few steps to a large tree to empty my bladder. I had a small flashlight in my bag, but the night sky provided enough light after my eyes adjusted.

Suddenly a cat dashed through the brush very near me. Then another cat jumped out further to the left. As I looked toward the sound of the last cat running, I could make out the shape of the plastic containers in a small circle that housed some of the cats. I then noticed three sets of pinkish-orange glowing objects with slight movement. I first assumed the glowing objects were the reflection of three pairs of cat eyes. After watching the objects further (approximately 30 seconds) I saw that the glowing was some sort of eyewear worn by three human-like figures. As I knelt to watch I could see these figures were handling the cats, and the subjects were wearing very low reflective off-white or gray coveralls.

After about two minutes all three subjects turned their heads toward me. Thinking they might be animal control workers and not wanting to frighten them, I stood up and said, 'How y'all doing?' With no vocal response all three began moving towards me, instantly closing to 30 feet that separated us. Slowly again I spoke saying, 'What are you guys doing out here?' They continued moving towards me. I heard them talking or communicating in a strange whisper. I couldn't understand. I also noticed they were shorter than me. I'm 5' 10" and I'd guess they were 8"–10" shorter than me. I turned and ran. I then walked a circle around the area and noticed no vehicles or signs of activity." HH

In July 2018 I received an interesting account from Arizona:

"Back in the spring of 2016, a few of my friends were talking about their experience with some weird creature, in the desert southeast of Tucson near Vail, Arizona. The descriptions sounded a lot like Mothman, though this creature had no wings. I was skeptical, but I didn't want to doubt my friends because whatever this was had scared them. They said that they believed it was an alien being.

Later that year, in the winter, these sightings were far from my mind. I was visiting a friend who lived in Vail. I stayed over late that evening. At about 2 am I left their house to drive about 25 minutes down I-10 towards home. Driving about 50 mph, when approaching a rise in the road, I saw a silhouette. Before I even processed that I was observing something I soon realized that I had slowed and eventually stopped on the shoulder to get a better view.

It was about 20 yards or so away, standing almost in the middle of the road. Because of the rise in the road, I could only see this form from the hips up. It was very tall and looked human-like. It was extremely skinny, with long thin arms and skin that was dark, leathery, and dry, though there was a 'sheen' to the body. The eyes were a reflective red color. I couldn't tell if it was looking at me or not. There wasn't another car in sight at the time.

I'm usually very calm during emergencies, but I was rattled by this. I'm very interested in unexplained phenomena, but confronting this thing, the panic switch flipped. My mind is telling me to hit the gas, but I just sit there, staring at this thing. I looked down for a second, considering turning around and driving back to my friend's house. I put the car in first gear, looked back up and the being was gone. I immediately drove towards my house. I was shivering uncontrollably the whole way home. I pulled into the driveway, walked in the kitchen door, and became violently ill. I passed out in my bathroom.

I didn't wake until about 1 pm that day. I dragged myself off the bathroom floor and immediately went to bed. I was exhausted and just wanted to sleep. I rarely left the bedroom for the next 5 days. I had no appetite and it seemed like every bone on my body ached. One of my friends eventually came over and helped me into the living room. I ate a little bit, but I was still very tired and despondent. I didn't tell her or anyone else what I had encountered. I just said that I had the flu.

Do you have any idea of what I observed out in the desert? Have you heard of similar creatures?" ML

I contacted "ML" by email. I was later able to talk to her by telephone. She was reluctant to discuss this event and was somewhat fearful that this being may seek her out. The being didn't seem to be an apparition, and her description suggests that it was a corporeal being. It is interesting as to the number of bizarre cryptids and humanoids that are encountered in the desert. This event was no exception.

I received the next account in August 2018:

"As I was driving home on July 31, 2018, at 01:43 on Ohio State Route 13 north of Mount Vernon, Ohio, a 7–8 foot tall, skinny, humanoid creature ran across the road out of a corn field across into a soybean field (from an east to west direction). I noticed the creature in my headlights from 50–75 feet away as I was traveling at a rate of 55–60 mph.

As it came out of the cornfield, I immediately let off the accelerator, at first thinking it was a deer but then seen the creature walked upright. It had a slender body, arms, and legs with a small diameter. The hands and feet looked over-sized for its body proportion. It had a small neck with oval elongated head, being dark tan to light brown skin tone and had no body hair. The creature slightly turned its head towards my vehicle's headlights, and I saw the creature's black eyes and small mouth just open slightly as it continued to run across the road. It barely took 2–3 steps, and it was across the road at a tremendous rate of speed.

I was in total shock and thought I should check it out at first but then thought for a second and being uncertain of what I may have just seen, I had better get out of the area. I lost sight of the entity due to darkness. I am a 24-year retired USAF aircrew veteran with a top-secret security clearance. Not to be bliss but would someone please advise me on what I seen because it still and truly and frightened me." K

This incident was one of three unusual sightings that occurred in the Mount Vernon, Ohio, area within a two-week period. Another described a velociraptor-like creature seen in the surrounding woods, and a third encounter was reported to be a shadowy humanoid observed in a woman's basement. Very strange series of events.

The following account was forwarded to me in January 2018:

"I work as a hospice chaplain and had a patient for about a year, that had no mental issues associated with her illness, that told me a tale a few times without wavering. In Grassy, Alabama, when she was a young mother, she was gathering laundry from the line and got a peculiar feeling before seeing this 3-foot-tall creature lumbering from behind the woodpile. It was white, had long stringy hair that dragged on the ground, and walked on all 4s. It had a long face like an armadillo with no fur on its face that was smooth like bone. It had kind eyes like a human and never broke eye contact. She froze as it approached. It got within hands' reach and then went 'flat like a bottom sheet' looking up at her. She quickly walked back towards the door. She also said that on that same night her baby was crying so she woke to tend to her and noticed the front yard was like daytime with sunshine and blue sky while the backyard was normal nighttime. This lady was a good honest Christian woman who has since passed." SB

The following encounter account was sent to me in January 2019:

"I live in Durham, North Carolina, in a standard two-story house in the middle of a run-of-the-mill neighborhood (lots of intersecting roads, etc.).

Two nights ago, my family was going to visit a relative who had given birth recently in Greensboro, so I had the house to myself. I was getting home at around 9 pm and decided to bring my dog in. She stays outside in the kennel for the day until we bring her in for the night. Our house has a garage attached to the left of it, and the garage has a back door that leads into the back yard. Her kennel is just to your right as you exit the door, with a 4–5 feet clearance/path in between it and the garage (there is also a bed of rock just up against the house, this will be important). She had recently been taken to the vet for her 'distressed' behavior, which is why I had to stay home to be with her.

The evening went fine. I watched a movie to pass the time. I then decided to take her outside before being put up for the night, around midnight. I took her out the back-garage door with her long leash (I was wearing socks and didn't feel like getting them soaked). She usually does her 'business' in that little clearing between the kennel and garage, so I let her walk down through it.

Our garage has a single light on the back wall (not LED or bright) so I can see her somewhat well while she does it. She's facing me when suddenly her backside lifts almost one or two feet into the air. (Paranormal or not I screamed at this). I assumed some wild dog, or something had tried to drag her.

She runs back to me, and I hear rustling among the rocks and this figure stops right as it enters visible view in the light. I've never seen anything like it in my life. 'It' was tall. I'm 6′2″ and I had to look slightly up to see where I thought its head was. It was pale but not white or grey, just normal pale flesh color (like someone who spends a week or two indoors). It was lanky, not anorexic or anything but disproportionate. It looked at me for a good 5 seconds before it backtracked in the quickest manner that I could never replicate. As soon as it left, I booked it back inside.

I was torn about calling the police if neighbors who had heard my scream hadn't. Behold almost half an hour later the police arrive in my driveway (I told them that I had seen a man in the back yard, leaving out the whole tall demon-like stuff going on).

Once again, I don't count myself as a 'believer' in the Bigfoot or Mothman but I don't know WTF happened. I'm most definitely not taking the dog out alone anytime soon.

What the hell was that thing? Why was it in a suburban neighborhood? Should I bother telling my family when they get back?" TS

This next incident report was received in September 2019:

"When I was 13, I was on an ATV with my two older sisters, one 15 and the other 18. We were going to my grandma's which was less than 2 miles away from my parents' place. We were traveling through our fields, but on the way, I suggested we go around the fence, so we didn't have to open the gates. It was pretty much the same path just a bit off to the side, we had gates because this was our pasture for the cows.

As we get to the middle of the field, we all noticed something sitting on top of the hill we were about to climb. On the top, there was a big pile of rocks from working the fields a long time ago. We slowed to a crawl because it looked human, we thought maybe a calf fell and was stuck, or maybe it was my uncle who looked after the cattle. But this thing's sitting position was odd. We were trying to figure out what we were seeing when this thing slowly stood up and my heart sank. Its arms were long, grossly long. I screamed and instantly jumped from the front of the ATV to the driver seat, replacing my sister. As we were switching this thing started running at us, but it was running weird. Its arms were swaying back and forth like a normal runner, but because of how long the arms were, it looked quite strange. You would think it would run on the long arms, but it didn't. It was running fast. I turned around and shot off straight through the field. My sisters were screaming it was still coming but I honestly could not look back at this thing, I just said don't look at it. We rounded the corner and that's the last we saw it.

As we got home, I crashed the ATV into the deck trying to get in as fast as we could. We were so scared that my parents believed us. They called all the family to warn if it was a trespasser. They said nobody had seen anything or anyone in the fields. Now I want to describe this thing, it was tall, skinny, and wore no clothes. Just a body is what we could see, pale grayish color, and the head wasn't shaped like a human head. We were about 30 to 40 yards from this thing. It was during the day too, that happened near Minot, North Dakota." SA

The next account was forwarded to me in October 2019:

"I witnessed a tall, pale-skinned being in my grandparents' yard in Willow Creek, California, in 1994.

My grandparents (dad's father and stepmother) lived in Willow Creek until their respective passing in the early 2000s. Before then my dad, sister, and I would visit at least once or twice in the summer and sometimes for a Thanksgiving or Christmas. We lived in San Jose, CA, at the time, which is an 8-hour drive away. We loved going to hike in the surrounding forests and playing in the Trinity River. We grew up hearing about Bigfoot (the famous Patterson-Gimlin film was shot in the area and the town is Bigfoot tourist-heavy), but we were taught to watch out for real mountain lions and bears.

I need to explain a bit about how my grandparents' house was laid out for some aspects of this story.

They had a small 2-bedroom, 1-bathroom house set at the corner of two streets. The road into the neighborhood off the main road ran along the back yard and the house ran along the other road off that road. Several houses ran each side of the street and a house sat behind their yard. Chain link fencing six feet tall went around their back yard and most neighbors' yards instead of solid wood fencing, so you can see into most yards. From the street and their house, it slopes down into the back yard and neighbor's yard by roughly 10 feet in total. Their back yard was mostly just grass and weeds with a small semi-growing garden near the neighbor's fence line and a big oak tree next to and partially over the solarium. They had a raised deck running the length of the back of the house with stairs down into the yard at one end and a solarium off their kitchen at the other end. Inside the house, the kitchen and dining room are immediately next to each other with the living room and front door next to it. At the back of the living room is a short hall with a master bedroom behind the kitchen and along the wall with the deck on one side, and the bathroom and guest room along the wall facing the side street on the other side. My grandparents of course got their master bedroom, dad would take the guest room, and my sister and I would sleep in the living room in winter or in the solarium if it was summer.

This story takes place in mid-August 1994. One last summer trip before school started in a few weeks at the request of my sister for her 9th birthday earlier that month. I was 11 at the time. We left early to get there before dinner so dad could nap from the drive a bit while my sister and I went down to the portion of the Trinity River that ran at the very back of the neighborhood. The afternoon and evening went as usual. That night, we went to sleep in the solarium as was the custom for summer trips.

At some point in the night, I woke up. No real reason, not even to go to the bathroom. I just have always done that from time to time, even still. I did what I usually do and stared up at the stars and moon (around half visible, couldn't tell you if it was waxing or waning). Suddenly, I got an intense feeling of dread that skipped fight or flight to straight 'freeze or you're dead' mode. After some time (most likely just a minute or two), I turned my head to the side and looked at the yard. I had to turn to my side and lift myself a bit to get a better look, but the source of my feeling was impossible to miss. Standing at the bottom of the yard next to the neighbor's fence line stood a tall skinny creature with skin the color of the moon. It had no hair on its head or anywhere else that I could see. Its eyes were shiny white with a reflective quality, but not like a bright light was shining on them right then. Just moonlight. Its face had human features but seemed closer to the face. Its arms were long, but that could be just because it was very tall. The chain link fence came up to its armpits, so it had to be around 7-8 feet tall. Not enough to just step over the fencing, but I didn't hear it climb over unless it had been in the yard before I woke up and just didn't get the dread feeling until later. Its body had dirty dark gray-looking rags over its chest and around its hips that covered its crotch.

It was looking right at me. I got scared and ducked down into my sleeping bag as far as I could. My sister has always been a heavy sleeper and I didn't want her to wake up for this anyway. Next thing I hear are heavy steps on the deck coming towards the solarium. There's a wood door with a screened window (not opened at the time as far as I can remember). All was quiet for a while, so I peeked out through a small fold of the sleeping bag. Through one of the bottom windows of the solarium next to the door, I saw its pale large feet. The skin was rough, and the toes were gnarled with dirty nails. I curled up trying not to make a sound or move much. The bag was getting stuffy.

Next thing I know my dad is gently moving me with his foot asking if I was cold because I was still huddled down into the bag. I looked around kind of disoriented. There was no evidence of that creature from the night before. No marks or footprints or bent fencing. My dad was a HUGE skeptic of anything paranormal, cryptid, and otherworldly, but I told him anyway. He of course blew it off as a dream. Sis, being a deep sleeper, didn't notice anything. I asked my grandparents if they heard or felt the thumping on the deck, which would have been along their bedroom wall. Nope. Both seemed weirded out by my story and my grandma later privately told me, 'There are lots of strange things up here. That's why we avoid being out at night.' She wouldn't elaborate though.

It's obviously not a classic Bigfoot, but I don't know what it was. I've wanted to ask someone from the Hoopa Native Americans up there, but I haven't yet. I've never seen anything like it since." AD

These tall pale humanoid sightings have been known to take place in areas where Bigfoot and upright canine sightings have occurred, so there may be a connection. Very interesting story.

This next detailed report was referred to me in November 2019:

"To provide some context, this incident took place about a year ago in November 2018, near my home in Michigan. I live about an hour away, north of Detroit. A used-to-be small town that's become more densely populated over the last decade, with a lot more hustle and bustle. However, where I live, I'm at least one mile away in all directions from any commercial zones or more modernized residential areas that tend to be a bit congested. It's one of the last stretches of slow, old farm country in the town that hasn't been overrun with cookie-cutter subdivisions.

My house was built in the 1970s by my grandfather, with whom I still reside, along with my husband, daughter, and aunt (we are his caretakers, while we save up and finish school to afford our own home). There's a sizeable lot of land between our house and our neighbors on either side. It might be worth mentioning that growing up, my friends always said my house looked like a house you'd see in a horror film, due to its setting amongst dense trees.

So, it's an autumn Sunday evening and the sun had been down for a bit. Most of the leaves had fallen by now but I recall it being an unusually 'warm' night, for that time of year. Everyone in my house was winding down for the night and preparing for the work/school week. I'd say around 10:30 pm, I decide to let my dogs out one last time before turning in for the night. I go to open our back door, which is a giant glass sliding door-wall window, and my dogs are right at my feet behind me, ready to bust out of the door as soon as it opens wide enough. I'm glad I didn't let them out because I guarantee if they saw what I briefly did, they would have both charged toward it and it would have just been bad news.

I open the door and where the edge of our yard ends and the brushy field begins (keep in mind, this brush is a bit taller than I am, I am five feet tall exactly) a pale, greyish figure is standing amidst the brush at the edge of the yard. The only reason I noticed it in the first place was that the noise my door made seemed to have startled it, so it made noise in the dry, fallen leaves, which then caused me to direct my attention towards this noise. Which is when I saw it, fleetingly, duck down and take off further into the field behind my house. It's difficult to describe but due to what I saw, being familiar with coyotes, feral cats, and other animals I'm used to seeing around the property, it had remarkably 'human' characteristics, given its height and how it crouched over before moving in bound-like strides into the field. Another thing I noticed was that it didn't make the sound of what a human would, or any animal that is native to this area for that matter would make in retreat. The pace wasn't quick, multiple steps like a human, deer, or coyote. They were lengthy, bounding strides. And the sound it made hitting the ground had weight to it. The tread was not light, I guess that is what I'm trying to say. It sounded big.

It kind of took my breath away and I was left startled myself but due to what I did see, believing what I saw to bear resemblance to a human, I sheepishly call out, 'Hello? Is someone out there?' I'm still standing in my doorway, kind of frozen in mild fear. I yell again, 'Hello?' This time, a bit more confident and enunciated. This captures the attention of my husband and my aunt. My husband comes downstairs to see why I was yelling outside, as did my aunt. I explain to them, kind of frantically, what I had just witnessed. My aunt was spooked, and my husband went upstairs to get a flashlight and his air rifle (I am an animal lover, and I don't like the idea of him shooting any animals, even problem animals, with something that can do serious damage like a 'real gun' so he uses an air rifle).

My husband and I both go outside into the back yard, him with the rifle and light, we begin scanning a pitch-black, overgrown field to no avail at first.

Maybe after five minutes of looking, my husband hops on top of his sedan that's parked outside to get a better view of the field or any movement through the brush and continues looking. His gaze stops in one direction though. He hops down and quietly approaches me in the yard and points in the direction of what he was looking at. About 20 yards into the field, in the direction closer toward the back of my neighbor's property, there are two glowing orange-red eyes looking right at us through the brush. Somewhat low to the ground.

When he gets me to see what he's seeing, he decides to shoot in the general direction of this thing to maybe startle it a bit, to see how it moves. He did this several times and it didn't flinch. Then he decided he would try to aim his fire directly at it, to get a reaction, and he's a very good shot. He hits it in what I imagine to be the face, and it sort of jumps up, and when it landed, it was a solid sounding thud against the ground. All the while, it did not break its gaze on us. After hitting the ground, it moved further back into the field without 'running away' necessarily, it kept eye contact with us the entire time. Almost as if it was walking backward, not once averting its gaze. It eventually moved far enough back that we both had to jump onto the car to still be able to see it. After several minutes of this, it had moved beyond our visual, so we hopped down and went inside.

It's worth mentioning that there wasn't any sort of light that would cause reflective eyes, aside from the moon which wasn't even full, and it was very dark. We purposefully kept our lights off and the eyes looked as though they weren't even reflecting light but more so emitting it.

Do with this what you will but my husband and I both know what we saw and given the frequency and variety of animals we see normally otherwise, this was significantly different than what we see. We have deer, coyotes, foxes, possums, raccoons, skunks, and feral cats, all of which we are very familiar with.

We have not seen anything like this prior to or since this time. Although we do hear strange sounds and noises in the field and the woods from time to time at night. My husband has woken me up in the middle of the night to listen to some strange moans and wailing, but that hasn't happened since earlier this year.

I felt it was valuable to share in the sense that not all encounters are ones where whatever it is, is inherently malevolent or predatory, in torturous pursuit of humans. It was just an experience that struck me as particularly odd." SG

The following account and sketch were provided to me in January 2020:

"We saw something we can't explain. About a year ago (2018), I was out back with my family. It was around 8 pm and the sun was setting. We lived in a farmhouse in the middle of nowhere, the closest neighbor was far away. Something down the field kept catching my eye, but I ignored it at first. My sister saw it too and kept looking out towards the trees. She was getting freaked out about it. My mom said to go investigate, so my sister and I started to walk across the field towards the tree line. Big mistake.

It's hard for me to describe. This was the most terrifying thing that has ever happened to me. I didn't see it at first and I didn't understand why my sister was so scared until we were about 100 yards away. Then I saw this creature. Tall, probably 8 or 9 feet tall. White, humanoid with an elongated head and no face. It had long arms and peeked around the trees. We stopped in our tracks. We couldn't tell what it was. It took a few steps further out of the trees and swayed back and forth at me like a praying mantis!

My sister and I ran screaming back to the house, where my mom stood, jaw dropped. She saw it too. I had never been so scared in my life. We grab the binoculars and watch this terrifying creature peek in and out of the tree line, spying on us. My grandma thought we all had a wild imagination. The sun was almost gone now, and it was getting dark, and the darker it got, the more it moved. Back and forth among the trees. It was terrifying, so we went in for the night and locked everything.

I couldn't sleep that night. I was hearing scratching on the roof, and at one point, a very loud bang and various noises coming from the barn. I was very afraid that I would wake up to my animals missing. The next morning my grandma asked if we heard the loud bang outside that night. She ended up taking my grandpa with her on her morning walk. I have no idea what it was, and it haunts me to this day. I was in Northwest Missouri. I believe it to be both paranormal and physical, it was a scary in-between. It was hard to look at.

I believe it wanted us. I was so afraid to look out the window, and I still am. Afraid to see that blank face on the other side of the glass. And on almost every night, the crickets would be chirping and there would at least be other animal noise and movement. But on this night, the world was dead silent and still. It gives me chills just talking about it. I do believe this creature was demonic.

I left this bit out because it's hard to explain, but you know how heat distorts light? Like on a hot day, opening a car door, releases heat and it casts a slight shadow on the ground. It felt like I was looking at a mirage. Like water that's not there on the road miles in front of you. But close. I would have thought it was a hallucination if everyone else didn't see it too. It was not hot outside, and it was getting dark. The shadows around it were moving, getting closer. Maybe it was the adrenaline or fear making me see things like that. But I do know the thing was real, and it came to the house that night. We could hear it outside and on the tin roof. I'm moving back to that farmhouse by the end of the month. I'm hoping not to see anything like that again." MM

Sketch that the witness provided.

The following incident took place in downtown Chicago and was reported to me in March 2020:

"I've had experiences before this incident, and I still doubt as to what I saw. This happened two summers ago (2018) in downtown Chicago.

If you've ever been to downtown Chicago during the summer after working hours you know how crowded it can get. I've been living here for 13 years, and I've seen my share of homeless weirdos. I commute using the subway each day and I have seen some weird people. The city has many and at first, that's what I brushed this sighting off as.

I was walking to the comic bookstore coming up to State Street. There's lots of shoppers and tourists going about their business when I saw what I will refer to as a homeless man on a corner on his knees. It was only when I looked at him again that I was confused. He looked like a Caucasian man that had a scar on his face that made him look a little deformed. He was wearing an oversized hat, but I could see he was bald. He was on his knees and muttering, something partially covering his face. I've never stared at someone before but there I was in the middle of State Street shocked and confused. He didn't look normal. His eyes were huge, and I felt sorry for him. His facial expressions just had lots of sorrow.

I looked around to see if anyone had noticed him. A young boy in his teens with his dad was looking at this thing the same way I was. I heard his dad tell the young boy not to look at him, but I could see the boy was also in shock and confused. He also knew that wasn't a human. Something about this humanoid was not right. Everyone else who walked by dared not look and ignored this humanoid. It was my signal to cross the street and I walked away but I kept turning around to get a glimpse.

The last thing I remember that was odd was how his eyes blinked. It reminded me of Smeagol from *The Lord of the Rings* movie. He didn't look real. I think about this sighting a lot and sometimes brush it off as it was just a weird-looking homeless human. The more I recall the sighting the more I'm convinced it was not a human. That's exactly what this thing was doing. Trying to hide in plain sight in front of hundreds of people. Its mannerisms were strange too. The way its head bent down but occasionally looked up to make eye contact was bizarre. It almost felt like I was looking at a wild animal at a zoo." AC

The next incident report was received in March 2020:

"I saw this creature in Vermilion, Ohio, in early 2012. I was at a friend's house around 4 am and was walking home. I saw a cop sitting at my local Drug Mart and it was past curfew, and since I was around 15 years old, I walked under the bridge onto a trail by our YMCA. I did this to walk through the woods and pass the cop so I could make it home. I was texting my friend while walking.

I had heard rocks being shuffled on the train tracks above, so I looked up and as my eyes were adjusting to the darkness, I saw this creature. It had cleared two 10 ft ditches running bipedally up a hill onto an abandoned gravel clearing. It was no more than 60 ft in front of me. It covered the distance within 4–5 seconds, cleared the 2 ditches up the hill through the gravel, and disappeared into the woods without making a sound. After it entered the tree line, I turned on my phone flashlight while walking up to the edge of the woods. It had completely disappeared. I describe it as 7–8 ft tall, hairless, skinny appendages, oversized feet and hands, inhumanly fast, oval head.

I had to continue through the woods for about 5 more minutes, completely terrified with every hair on my body standing up like needles. I got chills reading that someone experienced the same creature I did. It thankfully didn't stop to look at me like in the Mount Vernon State Highway 13 sighting. I couldn't see any facial features as my eyes were readjusting to the darkness from my phone light. Nevertheless, it was the most frightening encounter I have ever had." DG

The following account was received in April 2020:

"I was walking late one night with my German Shepherd when I smelled an overwhelming stench of roadkill. I looked over into the woods near my home and saw a naked pale white man-like thing crawling in the woods. It was on its hands, feet, and knees about 3 inches above the ground.

I changed hands with my flashlight which my dog's leash prevented me from immediately shining it in that direction. In the 2 seconds it took to change hands and shine the light on this thing, it had moved 20 feet to near a tree it was trying to hide behind. It saw my light as it was swinging towards it and quickly crunched into a cannonball-like posture and balanced on its toes & balls of its feet, hiding its face, and held perfectly still.

I got an overwhelming feeling that if I kept shining the light on it, that it would look up at me with glowing eyes and a weird face. So, I continued with my walk. I thought maybe it was a teenager doing a mime, but there was no one taking a picture and this thing had an oddly pronounced spine and was hairless.

I went home and looked on the internet to see if this is something kids are doing now (painting themselves white, shaving all hair off, rolling around in roadkill, and crawling around late at night in woods). Well, I found a picture on YouTube of a creature that a hunter's camera had taken that looked remarkably like this thing. I have no idea what it was. I live in a country suburb of Tampa, Florida, called Lithia. If you have any idea what this thing was, please let me know!" JK

The next witness recalls a yearly summer trip to the mountains in Potter County, Pennsylvania, when they saw a bizarre white humanoid walking around the trailer at night. The report was received in April 2020:

"I'm recounting something from when I was 14 years old. This was around 2013 or 2014. My family took a yearly summer trip up towards Ulysses, Pennsylvania, in Potter County (north-central PA) where there's nothing but woods, mountains, and forests. We owned land there, a part of a mountain where there were trails, fields, ponds, lots of animals, and dense shrubs. We stayed there for a week or more each year. We were all in a few different trailers spread out on this giant property and showered under spring water whenever we needed to.

I remember the entire day vividly. A few extra family members joined us. I recall that one of my cousin's friends came up and had a crush on me even though she was like 17. All the other kids and I played hide and seek in the field across from the main trailer where we ate and slept. It was a fun day. We saw some animals and got some scrapes and our legs hurt from running around so much. Ended up getting to be night quickly and there was a fire pit directly by the pond, so we gathered around and threw trash into the fire from our food boxes, plastic, etc. I think a few people left in the middle to go smoke a joint. So, it was me, another kid, and all the adults.

After an hour or so I ended up saying that I was going

back to my trailer because I was tired. I shared a room with a cousin, and I slept next to the window, and he was on a cot on the floor. I kept the window cracked because it was very hot in the trailer and even that slight breeze made me feel a little bit better.

I do wish I had never opened the window and gone to bed. I was finally dozing off around 2:30 am but I heard footsteps outside of the window. They were close. I assumed it was the other kids that went to smoke a joint getting back, so I ignored the footfalls. But they were strange because I remember it was as if someone was sneaking around and was slowly putting one foot in front of the other. It sounded like that except for loud steps, not sneaky at all, just slow and unnerving.

Twenty seconds later, I heard them again. As if whoever it was had circled the trailer. They stopped again. I heard a weird scratching noise as if [it] was coming from the far end of the trailer and twigs snapping farther up the hill outside the window. My heart was literally pounding from the sound of my cousin snoring, and the third time this thing's footprints were outside the window and somehow seemed like it was getting closer to the trailer each time. I expected this thing to come by the window again in its 20-second intervals and consistent movement since it'd already done it a few times.

I finally ended up peeping my head up from bed and pushing my eyes against the screen of the window. I remember looking in the direction it would come. I waited for it, and it seemed like a whole minute but there were no more footprint sounds. Absolute dead silence. Even my cousin turned and stopped snoring. No wind. Nothing. I lay back down, my heart was still beating hard.

Then I heard it again. The same slow, heavy two-foot walk. This thing stopped right in front of my window. I moved as quietly as possible back up and pushed my head against the screen again. I saw this thing, it was all white, it had all the facial features we have but its head was a strange cylinder shape, with a large bump on its head and no ears at all. It faced the way it would've gone if I had continued listening. I can't forget it! It never looked at me, so I didn't see its eyes. It just stood there facing that direction for a solid minute and I was watching it from behind the screen the whole time. This thing was frozen in place for a whole minute. No movement until I watched it bend its neck away from me and it started walking up the hill away from the trailer. The way it walked away was terrifying. The same bizarre walk and its arms opened and were so long they reached its knees.

That entire night ended with me falling asleep at 4:30 am with the window shut and sleeping next to my parents in another room. I went out the next day to check for footprints but there were none on that side of the trailer which made the experience even more terrifying for me.

My family asks me to go up there again, but it's 6 years later and I'm never going there ever again. I just say that I'm busy with work and school." ET

The next account involves a pair of humanoid encounters. The witness later observes a tall being creeping through a Minnesota forest while camping with his family. This was received in April 2020:

"My first sighting story is actually from an old friend of mine who I haven't seen or spoken to in years, but I still remember this very vividly to this day. It must have been about 1996 and I had just turned 22. I was at a party with a few friends, and the host of the party was the daughter of some wealthy family. She was a bit of a spoiled girl from what I can remember, and her parents had this really amazing house which I remember having this awesome chandelier at the entrance and one of the highest ceilings I've ever seen. Anyway, the house was in solitude and was the only house around for some distance. To get to it, you had to drive a minute or two along this long road that wasn't lit at all. The house was surrounded by a lot of forests but had a small lake nearby.

Now the party had been going on for a few hours and a buddy of mine was showing up late because of work or something. I have no idea why because it was years ago, but I know he showed up late. I remember being in the kitchen talking to someone and he bursts into the room fully out of breath and immediately comes to me and interrupts my conversation. He was extremely hysterical, and I remember telling him to calm down and breathe. He then began to say that his dad dropped him off where the long road began, as his dad was in a hurry. I remember thinking why the hell his dad would let him walk across a dark forest road to a secluded house at night on his own but who am I to judge someone else's family.

My friend was saying he was walking up the road about halfway when he heard a sort of growl behind him. Thinking he was about to get attacked by a wolf or whatever he began to walk at a much faster pace, and it wasn't until he turned around and about 10 feet from him at a tree was this hunched creature. I remember him constantly calling it this tall white thing. He said it had a huge head and gaping mouth. He let out a scream and then ran as quick as he could to the house. He made it to the house and busted in without looking back, which he then immediately found me. Now at the time and for years after I personally thought he saw an animal and his imagination went wild. I think people would just go, 'Yeah, dude, whatever.' But he never let anyone get to his head and he was always defensive over what he saw.

Now to my story and why I now believe my friend. I was camping with my wife and daughter in Minnesota last year at the beginning of July. For summer, the campsite we were at was quiet but there were [a] few families near our tents. It's next to a river and is covered by a thick forest. Now the opening of our tent faced north towards the river. It was a truly awesome view coming out of your tent. It was close to sunset but was still fairly lit enough to see across the river clearly.

I remember specifically saying to my wife that I needed the lighter to start the stove to boil some water for dinner. Now I remember setting up the stove and as I looked up to get a glimpse of the river something caught my eye. There was this thing, walking through the forest on the other side of the river. It was incredibly tall, and its limbs were so skinny. It didn't seem to look in my direction until someone from another family at our campsite shouted (not about the thing across the river, just about something else). That shout made it look over in my direction and I still remember its pale bulbous head looking straight at me. It then hunched over on all fours and began to crawl away at an incredible speed in the opposite direction.

I didn't sleep AT ALL that night. I didn't tell my wife or daughter because I didn't want to terrify my daughter because I know it would freak her out. The next day we were supposed to stay another night, but I didn't let that happen. My wife asked why, and I let her know what I saw. She knew I wasn't lying. Trust me, she would know if I was.

That creature still gives me the creeps to this day. It has given me a few sleepless nights. But finding out how many people have seen exactly what I've seen has helped me a bit." G

Here is another account that I received in April 2020:

"I'm from Alexandria, Kentucky, and I saw something that I couldn't entirely explain. On that night, it was 'Midnight Madness' for our school. It's some stupid football event during the summer but everyone goes to see people they haven't seen recently. I went with my two friends and one of their girlfriends.

We got there around 10:45 pm. I and my friends were getting bored of the event, so we left. We were driving around this sub-division that had very thick forests all around it. We settled on this abandoned house and decided to smoke some weed in the woods behind it. We had parked a little bit down the street so no one would be suspicious. I had left something in the car and decided to [go] back for it.

While I was walking back, I heard scratching from behind a nearby house. It kind of freaked me out but I thought it must have been a dog or an animal. I made it to the car and started heading back. As I was walking by the house, I heard the scratching. I began to hear it again but then I heard what sounded like a footstep kicking up gravel when someone starts trying to run. I turn and see something that has kept me up for many nights.

Now I'm a 6'2" 17-year-old guy so I am bigger than most people. And this thing that I saw had me easily beat in height by 2–3 feet. It was slender but with long almost stretched-out limbs. I couldn't really make out any more details because it was dark. The creature was running from one backyard to another. I never saw its face only its body. It ran on 2 feet, but it was faster than any person I have ever seen run. Hell, it was faster than anything I've ever seen. The creature made it from one backyard to the next (about 50–90 feet) in less than 5 seconds. I was standing in the middle of the street about 30 feet away. I stood there in complete shock. Then I ran as fast as I could to my friends. I ran through thorns and bushes to make it back to them.

When I reached them, I told them what I saw. I'm not too sure if they believed me but the panic in my voice was enough for them to know I had seen something unusual. We all ran back to the car. I have been trying to find out what I saw. The two closest things I have seen on the internet are the 'Dover Demon' [and] the 'Wood Devil.' I never saw its face so I'm not sure what it was. I was 100% sober when I saw the creature." PC

A Missouri boy and his family deal with a "Gollum-like" humanoid that continuously kills their chickens. I received this report in early spring 2020:

"I grew up in rural Missouri. My family moved there in 1985 when I was young. We were 15–20 minutes from the closest town, being Wright City, MO. It was in the middle of nowhere. You had to drive a mile or two down one gravel road, before you got to the gravel road I lived down. That was about a mile and a half long that only my family and our neighbor lived on. There was about 3000–4000 acres of land all around us that was owned by some guy who only came out during deer season to hunt the property south of us and lived in a town about 20 miles west. The land north of us was mostly incredibly hilly forest with a few caves about a mile north of a house. The land south of us was about 50/50 woods to fields with an old 100+ year old abandoned cabin deep into the woods. The wagon road to it had grown up.

The property owner had told us that no one had lived there since the 1800s.

I had a few sightings while growing up there. I had always told myself it was 'Momo, the Missouri Monster' (Missouri's version of Bigfoot). It wasn't until I saw a trail cam photo of what was said to be a pale crawler humanoid several years later. This prompted me to do a little more research.

My first memorable sighting was when I was a teenager. Me, my brother, sister, and dad were playing a game I learned in Boy Scouts called 'Manhunt' that was a blend of hide and seek and tag. We'd set a boundary around a cedar thicket just north of the house. Me and my little brother were on a team against my dad and sister. We played for hours. The cedars were thick, and the sun was beginning to set. We were probably in the last 10 minutes of daylight for the day.

Eventually I spotted what looked like 2 human-like feet about 30 feet in front of us. They were barefoot and pale. Not thinking much of it, I told my brother I thought Dad had taken his shoes off to be stealthier. We spread out about 20 feet apart and tried to sneak up on him from opposite sides. Crouching the whole way so we could see under the cedar trees, because we couldn't see through the thicket. We got about 15 feet away before it realized we were coming up on it and it took off. We both took off running after it thinking it was my dad. We chased it to the edge of the thicket where there was a small open glade before the start of the large forest that spread back into the hills. We yelled that he was running out of bounds, and as we got to the edge of the thicket, we noticed what appeared to be a pale naked man jetting into the woods. This spooked the hell out of my brother and me, but we still wanted to believe it was just my dad playing with us. So, we ran the opposite direction back south towards the house, only to see my dad sitting next to my sister by a pond easily 100 yards across the field from the thicket. We asked my dad how he got over there so fast, and he and my sister told us he'd been sitting there with her for 20 minutes waiting for us to figure out he wasn't in the woods. My brother and I tried to explain what we saw to him, but he blew it off saying it was probably just a deer.

Meanwhile, we had chickens at multiple times as I was growing up. Normally they'd be fine in the chicken coop for a few months, then something would start killing them. It was tearing open the wire fencing to the caged yard. Usually, we'd find 1 or 2 chickens just tore up and lying in the yard. My mom and dad always said it was wild dogs, but the chickens never looked eaten, just slaughtered. He'd always repaired the fencing, yet it kept happening. Usually once it started most of our chickens would be dead and gone within a week or two. My mom would be upset since she's the one that wanted to have chickens and would normally give up on them until the next spring when she'd get a couple dozen more. Sometimes she'd skip a year, but I can think of at least 4–5 occasions of getting batches of chickens and them all dying. Eventually she gave up and took a few years off from trying to raise chickens.

During my senior year of high school, she decided to try having chickens again. It was good at first. Then a couple months later, they started getting killed again. This time though it was peeling off the wire roof of the caged yard. The cage was about 5–6 feet tall. My dad said it was dogs, but the opening would normally be a few feet off the ground. I remember questioning my dad at that point saying if it was dogs, wouldn't they be trying to dig under the fence, not go in from the top? The slaughtering seemed to be worse than before with dead chickens being tossed all over the yard, yet just tore up, not eaten.

My sister had gotten a pygmy goat the year before to raise for FFA. One day we found it dead and mutilated as well. It was in a stable yard on the side of our barn with a 7-foot fence around it, yet something had still gotten to it. Parents still claimed it was dogs.

Then one night my sister's boyfriend was having a bonfire party and I went over there with my sister, because my parents wouldn't let her go to a party without me going with her to watch over her. My sister got drunk, but I didn't drink much because I was too busy watching over her. I think I had maybe half a beer all night. We left late, maybe one or two o'clock in the morning. When I got home, I would park my truck in the yard next to the driveway usually facing the chicken coop.

I pulled in and my sister just started screaming and pointing forward. I looked up and saw what at the time I could best describe as something that looked like the Gollum from *The Lord of the Rings* on the roof of the chicken coop. It was staring right at us, crouched down just like Gollum normally was in the movies. It was a pale white, it had very thin hair on top of its head, probably less than Gollum had in the movies. And it had 2 red eyes that glowed in the head-lights. It appeared to be hissing at us. I locked the doors and quieted my sister down, then started honking the horn and flashing between my high beams and regular headlights. Me and my sister were both freaking out. It jumped off the back of the chicken coop towards the direction of the woods north of the house and I lost sight of it.

My parents had turned on the outside lights at that point and were looking out the door. I grabbed my sister and ran as fast as I could inside with her. When we tried to tell my parents what we saw, they refused to believe us. They told us we were just drunk. I tried to tell them I wasn't drunk, but they wouldn't believe me. Sadly, my sister was so drunk, she didn't even remember coming home the next day.

A few nights later, we were all gathered in the living room to watch a movie we had rented from the video store. As we were watching the previews, we heard the chickens screeching. My dad was still convinced it was dogs and had a loaded .30-30 rifle by the back door ready for when they showed up again. He ran and grabbed his rifle and a spotlight also near the door and ran out back.

A few moments after he went outside, we heard a gunshot followed by continuously firing until he emptied the whole clip. This was very unlike him; growing up he taught me and my brother that a good hunter only takes 1 shot at something. If you need 2 or more, you're not a good enough shot. He even made us get our first kill with single load muzzleloader black powder rifles before we could use a regular rifle with a magazine. Never in my entire life had I seen or heard my dad unload a full clip at something.

He charged back in and immediately told us kids to go lock all the doors and windows to the house. He was white as a ghost. Meanwhile he said he needed to talk to my mom. He took my mom into the back room and closed the door where they were at for 20 minutes. I already knew what it was. I was already scared before he even went outside. Me and my brother and sister waited in the living room until they got done talking. I asked him what he saw, and he told me he didn't want to talk about it and not to bring it up again. The next day, him and my mom decided to slaughter all the chickens and that we wouldn't be getting more.

To this day my dad still won't talk about what he saw, and nowadays acts like it never happened and plays stupid.

"I went off to college a couple months later, and I never saw it again after that." JN

A young man and his uncle encounter a tall boney humanoid that was harassing the livestock in the barn. This occurred in a rural area of northern Utah and was forwarded to me in May 2020:

"It was mid-May several years ago, when my family took a trip down to my uncle's farm, in Utah, not far from Salt Lake City. About 90 miles, I'd say. The area was remote and several miles away from the nearest town. When we arrived, it was about 3:00 in the afternoon, and the sun was shining bright as ever. My uncle sat on the porch and waved to us as we pulled into the front gate. We usually go down there every 2 years and stay for about a week or two. It's pretty much the same back home in Michigan. The livestock, the fields, hot summers, it all feels like I'm at home.

At first, nothing seemed out of the usual. It was just your average 2 story farmhouse, with a big barn and sprawling fields for miles. It was peaceful. I got out of the car and got my bags out of the back. My uncle lived in Utah his whole life, so he has a bit of an accent. 'Hey there!' he shouted from his chair on the porch. 'Hey, Uncle Ron,' I said with a smile. 'How you been, boy?' I walked up the steps and set my bags by the door. 'Pretty good, how about you?' I asked. 'Well, I was about to go hunting, forgot y'all was coming today. You're welcome to come with me if that's alright with you.' I nodded. Hunting was normal in Michigan. I usually get a buck or two during rifle season.

'Hey, Mom, is it alright if I go with Uncle Ron to go hunting? We'll only be a couple of hours." She sighed and looked at us for a second. 'Yeah, that's alright.' She spoke. 'Here, you take mine, I'll go get another one.' He grabbed the rifle he had leaning against the wall and handed it to me. 'Make sure she ain't loaded,' he said before he headed inside. I pulled the bolt back slightly and checked if it was loaded. Once I saw it wasn't, I held it freely. 'You two better be back before 10:00, because we all know that your uncle likes to take his time,' she said as she walked up the stairs. 'Okay, Mom, I'll make sure.' Just as I said it, my uncle came out the door, letting the screen door slam behind him. 'Alright, let's get going,' he said. 'I told the boy to be back by 10' said my mom, before my uncle walked off the porch. 'Will do,' he said with a smile.

Behind his house was a thicket of woods. Had to be about 100 acres. We entered the tree line, bright-eyed and bushy-tailed, ready to get ourselves a buck. He had a blind about a quarter mile in, so we had a little bit of a walk. And as we did, I felt eyes on us. It was unnerving, but I didn't think much of it. Once we made it to his blind, we got inside and zipped it up. The time out in the blind was very uneventful, until about 9:00. The first thing we heard all day was the scratching. I and my uncle looked at each other, and he whispered, 'It's gotta be a buck rub.' Right as he said it, the scratching stopped, and my uncle raised his gun.

He looked out of the hole in the blind, only to see nothing. 'Don't you think we should head back?' I whispered. He checked his watch, then nodded. 'Yeah.' We both got out of the blind and made our way back home. I felt eyes on me again. This time I asked my uncle if he felt them too. 'It's probably just nothing,' he said. I shook it off and relaxed a little. We got back to the house at about 9:30, right after the sun had set. I walked up the steps to the house and walked in. My mom was at the table, talking to my aunt Denise. She looked over at us and smiled. 'Hey, guys, how was it?' she asked. 'Uneventful,' I said. My uncle walked in behind me. 'I'll take the gun,' he said. I handed it to him, and he walked upstairs.

'What did you come back for?' asked my mom, looking at

my uncle. 'What do you mean, you said to be back by 10,' he said. 'No, I mean earlier, I heard you open the barn door. I looked out the window just as you went back into the woods,' she said, confused. 'We didn't go in the barn,' I said to her. She looked at me with a look of confusion. 'Huh?' said my aunt. 'You didn't come back?' 'No, we were in the blind the whole time,' said my uncle. Then it hit me. The sudden realization that something was out there with us.

My uncle opened his mouth to say something, but before he could, he was interrupted by the squealing of the pigs out by the barn. He always kept his rifle with him outside. 'Go out to my truck and grab the shotgun off the rack. Might be a whole pack of coyotes out there.' He jumped up out of his chair. I ran to his truck, swung the door open, and grabbed his shotgun. It was a 12-gauge, slug round, nothing I was too aware of at the time. My uncle and I ran out to the barn.

We both froze in our tracks. What was out there, harassing those pigs, wasn't a pack of coyotes, but a damn thing from hell, or so it looked like. Boney clawed hands, skinny, with a boney rib cage. The damned thing seemed to stare into your soul, with its huge eyes. It loomed over us. It had to be about 7 to 8 feet tall. Out of sheer fear, I took a shot at it. And another. Before it took off into the woods. We stood there in shock. The pigs were squealing and running in circles. They were just as scared and confused as us.

I looked at my uncle. 'What the hell was that?' I asked. 'I'm not sure, but it had to be what your mom was talking about.' We checked the pigs, and a few had minor lacerations, but none of them were dead. We checked the area the thing stood but found nothing, not even blood. I've never wanted to leave somewhere more than right then. Once we got inside, my mom and aunt were eager to hear what happened. When we told them, they were as shocked as us. I had a hard time sleeping that night. Feeling that same feeling of being watched. The next day we left. I've only been back to Utah a couple of times, and my uncle hasn't seen anything out of the usual. But one thing for sure, I won't forget about that night." ZC

A woman is driving to a friend's house on Christmas night when she encounters a tall lean walking humanoid that screams as she passes by. This occurred in upstate New York and was received by me in May 2020:

"This incident occurred on Christmas night 2007 at our family home in upstate New York. The day was pleasant and festive; opening presents early in the morning with my sisters, hearty breakfast made by Dad, delicious smells from the kitchen as Mom and Dad prepared a feast, visits from extended family bringing pies and cakes for dessert. Around 2 pm we all sat down to eat and then lazed about for the rest of the afternoon into the evening.

At about 8 pm, after everyone had left and the food was all put away for round two the following day, I decided to head over to visit my friend in the next village. The drive would be about 10 minutes if I took the back roads to get there. So, I did.

First, a little background on where my friend lived. It was a housing development surrounding a private lake. You might call it a 'gated community.' You could still drive through it freely after hours by entering 1 of 4 private entry points. Since the community was built around a lake, the roads surrounding it went in a spiral sort of shape. The houses were sparsely positioned on the outermost part of the spiral road, closest to the 4 private entry points. As you drove in further, there were a lot more houses positioned closer together nearer the lake.

My friend lived on the outer edge of this development, so once I reached the entry point, it would only take me another few minutes until I reached his house. His house, along with all the others, were far enough apart that you couldn't see them from the road. As you drove by there were either woods all around with long drives, or open fields with long drives. You could see porch lights on in the distance but that was about it.

As I entered the development, the speed limit dropped from 30 mph down to 20. There were no streetlights in the development and for some reason, I never put my high beams on. I couldn't go any faster than the speed limit because there were speed bumps in place every 30 feet or so for a bit.

It was a mild night. I remember having my driver's side window open slightly taking in some fresh air. Driving in silence was unusual for me (I normally always listened to music when driving). I was enjoying the quietness after the commotion of the day.

I reached a section of road that had barren fields on either side and woods set back. Houses were probably nestled back into the trees. As I drove, I noticed what looked like someone walking up ahead on the opposite side of the road, coming in my direction. Mind you, I was still going about 20 mph the whole time, so it was probably less than a minute by the time the 'walker' came into clear view. I got a quick scan of it from my windshield before my car and it was exactly parallel. This is what I saw.

It was not a person. It stood on two long legs, with long arms hanging down from its shoulders. It was strong looking. Lean, muscular, but not beefy in stature. It looked thin at the same time. It stood at least 7 feet tall. It was light-colored, not sure whether it was white, tan, yellow, or greyish. It didn't appear to have fur but there was some texture to the skin that wasn't smooth. There appeared to be something coming down off its back. I don't know what this was. All I can recall about its face is the small features it had but the mouth and jaw were notably large. And it had pointed things atop its head; 2 things going straight upward with something mingled between the two things. That's what I got from a quick scan and my observation of it as it neared my car and my car neared it.

As my car became parallel to it within a split second, I went from looking out my windshield to looking at it from my driver's side window. At that moment, its face quickly peered down at me and all I remember was the mouth opened wide. Out came a remarkable scream that I'll never forget. Gives me the chills just thinking about it. It consisted of a high-pitched shrill/shriek, enveloped by a deep guttural growl. Both sounds happened simultaneously in that scream.

I kept driving all the while. This was all happening so fast that I didn't even have a chance to be scared or shocked or anything.

I continued driving and went past my friend's house and drove home. I called him to tell him what happened and that I just needed to get back. I was probably running on adrenaline to get back home. Later, I was in total shock after it sank in. Had my driver's side window been opened fully, it would have touched me, or worse, assaulted me. I'm certain of it.

To this day, I still haven't worked out what this was." DE

The next account was forwarded to me in May 2020:

"I'm not really into the paranormal, but I had an experience 13 years ago that I've never been able to explain. I want to ask for your opinion.

It was the fall of 2007. I was making the 2-hour drive home from my university along rural county roads in northern Minnesota. The roads along this route are paved and ditches are well maintained. The land just off the right-of-way is forested. For anybody curious, this was on County Road 58 near Two Inlets, Minnesota.

I was in a section of roadway with nice long winding turns. Very fun driving. It was just dark enough to need headlights to see. As I came around one of these winding turns the beam of my headlights caught a humanoid figure standing in the long grass in the ditch, maybe 50 feet in front of my car. As my car turned and my lights shone on it, the thing strode gracefully but quickly the 20 or 30 feet into the woods just off the right-of-way.

This thing was at least 7 feet tall, taller than a normal man, but standing naturally erect. It was not an animal on its hind legs. It was grey, with no hair, and very thin; thin enough to see joints. It walked so quickly and gracefully. I've never seen anything like it.

Wildlife typical to that area are bear, deer, rabbits, the occasional wolf, but I can't think of anything that explains what I saw.

After I saw the thing, I contemplated turning the car around to have another look or maybe find some tracks, but I was in full-on freak out mode, so I just kept driving. I was pretty shaken up when I made it home.

Do you have any ideas what I might have seen?

I'll state for the record that I am a Christian, and I've tended to wonder if I saw a demon or evil spirit. From the feeling it gave me, I certainly don't feel like I saw an angel." PS

A group of friends encounter a white crawler humanoid while camping on private property on a Civil War battlefield. This account was received in May 2020:

"I live on the East coast in central Virginia (Hanover County), and the property I live on contains 10 acres of fields and woods. Just some background info. The property was once part of a battleground during the Civil War. The Battle of Matadequin Creek took place right around where I live. My friends and I have always seen ghosts and paranormal activity around the property whenever we hang out or camp, but that isn't why I'm typing this.

I should probably mention that our campsite contains tarp roofs with pallets set up as walls. I should also mention that we always carry firearms with us in the woods, but I always enforce making sure nobody has any bullets chambered in their weapons unless they have a reason to shoot.

One night in late April 2020, three friends and I were hanging out by the fire within our campsite. At about 11:30 pm. One of my buddies and I wander down the trail with no flashlights of any sort in the dark. We stopped at an opening by the field where we could see the stars. We chatted about random topics for about 5–10 minutes until we start hearing steps and twigs snapping in multiple areas in front of us. We are skeptical but kept an ear out.

Suddenly, I'm startled and uncharacteristically rack a bullet in the chamber of my rifle as quick as I can. Then I immediately aim my rifle towards what I'm seeing. It was dark so I couldn't distinguish details, but this is what a saw.

It was a pale white silhouette and it was crawling uphill from another trail. It didn't seem intimidating though, rather intently curious. Its body moved like a chicken that bobs its head but more subtle. My friend and I yelled for our other 2 friends to come to assist us. As the creature got closer, we yelled louder. We weren't terrified, simply frightened and in awe. The creature went behind a tree and repeatedly poked its head out and back behind the tree. It occasionally began to crawl towards us from behind the tree but would retreat once again. All its movement was slow and agile. After about 2 minutes, it disappeared, as in we couldn't see it because of the brush. I assume it fled into the woods.

Our other 2 friends arrived a minute or so after the creature had fled. Their excuse was that they thought we had run into a hunter or somebody, so they decided to take the bullets out of their weapons.

The next day, we went back to the spot of the sighting. We found disturbed leaves and tracks exactly where we saw the creature. The friend I was with during the sighting is a skilled hunter and tracker. We followed tracks that led off the property until it seemed to either go cold, or we lost them. We did find a small-sized goat skull in the woods with no carcass to follow near the sighting area.

Does anyone know what this could be?" KK

I will attest those battlefields and other locations, where sudden death and destruction have occurred, seem to draw a variety of unexplained phenomena.

This next account was received in May 2020. Two sisters are chased by a tall skinny humanoid, which drops to all fours, while skateboarding at night in a nature park in Gulf Shores, Alabama:

"About five years ago my older sister and I went to a nature park, a wetland so to speak, in Gulf Shores, Alabama. Of course, we went at night so we could skateboard around because you aren't allowed to. But you know, a 14-year-old trying to look cool in front of her 24-year-old sister. Well, we went just around as the sun was setting.

For a little bit we got lost since the park was so huge and condensed with thick woods. We were trying to find the bridge, a 20 foot or so bridge so we can hang out just above the rushing river. By the time we got there the sun was hardly visible over the mountains. I looked around after drinking my water and here is where the creepy stuff happened.

As I looked at the other side of the bridge I saw a tall skinny human-like figure. I first shrugged it off like it was a person, maybe a ranger of the park. But then it got on all fours and walked away. I didn't say anything at first, mainly because I thought it was maybe a bear. I looked back at my sister as we chatted about boys and many other things. Then I looked back at the end of the bridge.

My sister did too, and we both saw the figure this time. At this point I was freaked out, mind you it's still not dark out, the sky was purple and orange, so it wasn't like we were seeing things like when your mind pictures figures in the dark. No. It was right there and getting closer.

I told my sister to get the hell out of there, her going first off the bridge and down the hill. I followed, and as I turned to look at the bridge again it was 5 feet in front of me on all fours once again. It stood there as me and my sister skated off and this isn't even the end.

I told my sister to head to the main building since there is cameras and lots of light. We skateboarded for what seemed like hours, every minute seemed to last eternity. As we finally get to the main building, we finally stopped riding our boards. Out of breath and scared we both looked around. By this time, it was pitch black outside. We made a mad dash to the car, taking a path we have never seen before, but it was outside the park which made us feel safer.

After we got to my sister's Jeep, we both got in, hearts racing and scared out of our minds. And when we tried to leave, the gate was locked. Meaning we couldn't leave since there was only one way in and out of the park. We got even more scared. We tried everything to get out. We even thought about just leaving the car behind and walking the 2 hours home. But we drove onto the sidewalk and got out of the park.

To this day I won't go back to those wetlands ever again. Even in daylight. Whatever that thing was I never want to see it again. I can't stop thinking about it. And I'm almost 19. You can think this is just a story, but it did happen. Me and my sister don't even talk about it to this day. Something changed between us, I could feel it after that day." DL

I received the next harrowing account in spring 2020:

"On a summer night at the end of July in 2008 we were camping while working to sell our wares at a flea market in Huntington, West Virginia. It was hot in the camper, so I got up and walked outside where I found my nephew sitting and texting on his cell phone. It was about three in the morning.

Deciding to take a walk in the night air we made our way about a hundred yards to the end of the long flea market building and sat down on a concrete slab. The light that was on top of the building illuminated the area where we sat. To our front there was a big open field, and behind the field there was a tree line that led to a forest. A large billboard on the highway cast a sliver of light across the ground but the rest of the field was pitch black.

As we sat there chatting, I saw something white about 80 yards away squatted down on the edge of the tree line. I looked at my nephew and asked if he saw what I was seeing. He said he did but neither of us could determine what it was.

The creature started to emerge from the tree line, it came out about twenty feet almost crawling to stay close to the ground. When it reached the edge of the sliver of light that was streaming across the field, it paused for a second, never breaking its gaze on us.

When it reached the edge of the light it leaped, elongating its body to move through the light in one movement, and landed in the darkness on the other side, still maintaining his stare. The time in the light allowed me to see it more clearly, its body was long, gangly, slender, and pale white. At this time, it was about 10 yards away from us, having cleared half the original distance. It started to inch closer, pausing in a stealthy, curious manner, inching toward us as we sat there shocked and frozen at the sight of it.

Now it is about three yards away and it stayed in that position for a longer time. At that point I had time to take in its features in greater detail. Its stature was 4–5 feet tall, very lean, and skinny, pale white skin with no hair on the creature at all. It kept itself in a hunched position when still. Its knees folded backward like an animal's hind flank. Its arms were long and skinny, reaching down to hands that had very long, thin fingers with claws.

It had big black, almond-shaped eyes, very small pointy ears that were close to its head. It had very long, pointed, interlocking teeth that were always exposed and lips that were so small they barely showed around the huge teeth. Its nose turned upward like a bat and lay close against its face.

Crouched, it slowly walked to the edge [of the] light we were enveloped in. Within two yards now. It was looking at us, making a low snarling sound as it breathed. That was all I could hear over the pounding of my heart, which was now in my throat. It was staring at us and cocking his head from side to side as if it was trying to figure out its next move.

As I sat there wondering what could happen next, it sprang into the light with its arms up and mouth open wide, making crazy, screaming, growling sounds running toward us. Coming to within a foot of us, I leapt to my feet, putting my fists up in a defensive posture. It looked up as if noticing I was larger than it originally thought. Then, it quickly turned and ran away, kicking dirt and gravel up in my face. It was off through the field, and I watched as it ran toward the forest. Then I heard the rustling of the brush as he moved through the woods." RE

Three servicemen are camping at Monjeau Lookout outside Ruidoso, New Mexico, when they encounter an odorous white humanoid that is circling them in the adjoining trees. I received this account in June 2020:

"Two of my friends and I used to be stationed at Ft. Bliss in El Paso, Texas. We decided a Memorial Day camping weekend would be a good idea; so, we took a trip up to Monjeau Peak outside of Ruidoso, New Mexico. We planned to stay for three nights, the first two of which were very relaxing. On our first day there when we were deciding where to set up our tent, we found loads of bones from various animals, not mounded up or anything like they were collected, just bones all around the campsite. The campsite had five places to pitch tents over about 300 square meters. We decided to pitch our tents on the highest point at the campsite, about 30–40 feet higher elevation than the parking lot.

On the third night, it was well after sunset when all noise from the woods died out. I'm not sure how long it was silent before me and my friends broached the subject. But it wasn't long after that that the hair on the back of my neck started to stand, followed by goosebumps all over. I could see my friends starting to get jittery, and from one of the other campsites, we heard their two dogs going absolutely nuts. These were very relaxed and happy dogs for the last two days. We had also made decent acquaintances with the couple who had the dogs and they had lunch with us on day two. The other two groups that were camping at the same time had gone silent as well.

The car was about 60 meters from our campsite, and we unanimously decided to go get our guns (AR-15s and 9mm pistols). On our way back we started to smell a rotting, fetid stench. I don't know if anyone has ever had to burn feces before, but it smelled like that mixed with death. It was cloying and felt like it was almost physical it was so strong. We got back to our campsite and decided to post [a] guard all through the night. One man up and two asleep, or at least resting. I volunteered for the first shift because I knew I wasn't getting any rest at all.

We had plenty of firewood for the night, especially because we were leaving the next morning. I kept the fire blazing as much as I could because I figured that if it was some sort of animal, it wouldn't be too interested in messing with me. I kept my back to the fire so I could maintain good night vision. The forest to the southwest of our campsite was pretty burnt out, but what you can't see very well is the elevation change. Once you got into the tree line it was very steep, not impassable by any means; but not somewhere you need to be walking at night. Behind the trees, I noticed a stark white shape. I shouldered my rifle, and it didn't move at all.

I assumed it was a tree partially hidden behind another one. I started scanning the tree line with a flashlight because I felt the stench was stronger than it was before. As my beam passed over what I thought was the obscured tree, I saw eye-shine from the white shape. As soon as I registered what I was seeing, it disappeared behind the tree. I debated investigating but instead just roused my friends, and we scanned together. When my shift ended, I took off my rain fly on my tent so I could see out if needed. I didn't see anything on my next shift, just the smell.

In the morning, just before dawn broke, the smell seemed to recede but only so much, almost like it left a scent as a warning was the impression that I got. We broke camp and started packing up. About halfway through our break down, we saw the other three groups packing up as well. I went over and talked to the couple with the dogs, asking them if they saw anything last night, or if their dogs calmed down after the barking stopped. They told me that even when they stopped barking the dogs didn't sleep. They spent the night whining and growling in the direction of the hill to the southwest." CE

Witnesses mentioning an overpowering stench attributed to these pale humanoids does occasionally occur.

The following account was forwarded to me in early summer 2020:

"Growing up in the mountains of North Georgia, camping and hiking were things I and my brother did so often it was second nature. So anytime Rob and I had a break from school we would head straight for the woods. We packed our gear, let our parents know where we were going and that was that, no questions asked.

We decided to camp about midways through Jacks River Trail in the Cohutta Wilderness and it's a trail we knew well, as we had used it a few times before to practice long hikes. We arrived at the trailhead around lunchtime, parked the car, got our gear out, and headed into the woods. We passed a few hikers as we moved along and asked them how the trail looked and the answer was always the same, 'wet.'

Jacks River Trail probably crossed the river fifty times as it went along its seventeen-mile-plus journey, and with the colder temperatures of late fall settling in, it was harder for the trail to stay dry. We moved deeper into the trail and started to look for a place to make camp. This is where Rob and I made our first mistake. You see, Rob and I have this rule. We don't camp near people if possible.

Call us paranoid but the last thing we want is for someone to drag us out of our tents and into the woods, never to be seen again. So, we always camped a decent way off the trail and in the area that wasn't popular with overnight camping.

Roughly two and half hours or so we found what we thought was the perfect place to set up for the two nights that we would be out. We came up to Horseshoe Bend and ventured about half a mile off the trail into a clearing and set up. We built a teepee fire lay for that night and pitched our tents on either side. After setting up and unloading we decided to walk back to the trail and go exploring around some of the many swimming holes Jacks River had to offer.

This was during Thanksgiving break, and I remember being surprised at how few people were on the trail. Maybe it was the weather or the fact that this was early in the week but there didn't seem to be anyone hiking much less staying the night. Around five o'clock Rob and I headed back to camp to start our fire, make dinner, and settle in for the night. As soon as the sun began to set, the cold rushed in. We added more wood to the fire, sat close, and just enjoyed the conversation.

Rob was two years behind me in school. I was a senior and he was a sophomore but growing up we had always been close. We always hung out in the same groups, played the same sports, had the same hobbies, etc. Around 9 pm we were settled comfortably around the fire. I had just texted our mom to let her know we were safe and getting ready for bed, and I remember we were talking about dreading going to our grandparents' house for Thanksgiving and having the same awkward conversations we had each year with family we only saw on holidays, when things started to get strange.

We were no stranger to sounds in the woods and these woods were full of animals, from deer to black bears and even the random wild boar. If you are in the woods enough, you learn to distinguish certain sounds, and what we were hearing I can only chalk up to as odd. What Ryan and I heard was what sounded like someone sneaking around slowly just out of eyesight. With an animal walking on four legs, you hear a tighter group of steps, but what we were hearing sounds very distinct to what a human sounds like when walking slowly or trying to move without making much sound.

I remember we both pulled out our flashlights and shone them in the direction we felt the sounds were coming from but that is what was so weird. Whenever we would fix our lights on a spot we thought the sound was coming from, the location of the sound would suddenly change.

It was as if multiple people were walking around us. That's when the whistling started. At first, I thought it was the wind and I remember thinking maybe the wind is just throwing leaves around and what we are hearing is nothing but the wilderness around us. Rob looked at me and asked if I was hearing that. I didn't answer and was trying to focus hard on each sound. Two consecutive notes with roughly a three to four-second gap and then two more consecutive notes. Repeatedly.

Rob kept asking if I heard that and I put my finger to my lips trying to keep him from talking. The fear I felt was incredible. My jaw was tight, my fist clenched, knowing I wasn't ready for whatever was out there if it was anything at all. The whistling continued for what felt like forever but thinking it through, was maybe five minutes when Rob finally yelled out into the darkness, 'HEY!' Quiet. The whistling stopped. The crunching of the woods stopped. Nothing. I was pissed. I looked at Rob with a 'what the hell' look and he shrugged his shoulders. 'I had to do something,' he said. I just shook my head.

We sat there in silence for a few minutes when the woods erupted with noise. Something or someone was running in a circle around our campsite. The whistling came back. Two consecutive notes with the same three to four-second gap and then two more consecutive notes. How could someone whistle this loudly without cracking while also running? I was done. I stood up, shining my flashlight in all directions trying to catch a glimpse of whatever was screwing with us. Nothing. It felt close enough to touch but we never saw a thing. That's when the movement stopped but the whistling was still constant.

It was so loud. Inhumanly loud. I looked at Rob and told him to call the police. Now, this is the part I will never forget. The part I never like to talk about.

While Rob was on the phone with a dispatcher and telling them our location and what was going on, I stepped around the fire towards my tent. Inside my bag, I had a six-inch fixed blade that I always carried and thought I would feel a bit more comfortable with it in my hand more than just my flashlight. As I went to unzip my tent, trying to keep my eyes toward the woods, I heard some movement directly in front of me.

I swept my light up in front of me and for maybe two seconds I saw it. Whatever this person or thing was, it was about five feet up in a tree. Everything about it was long. Its arms, legs, neck, fingers, everything. And it was fast. As soon as the light hit it, [it] launched backward, off from the tree. I heard it land but it either jumped an impossible distance or landed in a thicket because I heard it but never saw it.

I don't think I have ever yelled so loud. I ran back to where Rob was and sat down. He kept asking me what I saw but I couldn't answer. I just kept thinking about what I saw. Maybe ten minutes later we saw a couple of flashlight beams coming through the woods, and three guys came into view asking if everything was ok. I settled a bit and started asking them if they had seen or heard anything.

All they said was they heard a lot of movement and then heard my scream and that's when they headed in our direction. I tried to explain what had happened without sounding crazy, but it didn't seem to work. One of the guys walked around a bit and came back and said he didn't see anything. Rob told them that we called the police and roughly thirty minutes later a park ranger showed up.

Rob and I tried explaining everything to him, but he just chalked it up to either a curious animal or some campers trying to mess with us. Either way, Rob and I decided we weren't staying the night. We packed our stuff up and walked out of the woods with the ranger. He took our statement and we got in our car and drove home.

Rob and I don't talk about what happened that night but neither of us has been back to Jacks River Trail and will probably never go back." MA

Small crawling humanoids attack a house on the Navajo reservation in Arizona. It is believed that these shapeshifting entities were the result of a curse placed on the family several generations ago. This account was received by me in June 2020:

"My story took place several years ago when we lived on the Rez in Arizona. My entire family had gotten together for my mom's birthday and spent the night at my grandmother's house out in the sticks, in the middle of nowhere.

At about 10:30 pm her dogs started barking and howling like crazy. No one got up to check because it was pitch black outside. But I could tell that the dogs were running back and forth chasing something. I got curious, so I turned the outside light on and stepped out the front door to see what was going on.

Then suddenly, something jumped from the tree onto the side of my grandmother's house and started crawling like 'Spiderman' all around the house. It was hard to make out, but it looked like a small man crawling like a lizard. The house was made of stucco, but it moved around easily. This thing was fast too. The dogs were going nuts.

I ran into the house screaming. Everyone was terrified and I remember crawling underneath the bed. The noises were horrible, and it sounded like there were more than one. I heard squeaking sounds that got real loud at times. They would jump on top of the roof and could be heard walking around. I don't remember how long it lasted, but I was under the bed the entire night.

When dawn came, we all went outside to check out the house. There were a few bits of stucco knocked off, but not as bad [as] I thought it would be. The dogs were in the tool shed and too tired to move. Then my uncle got a ladder, so he and I climbed to the roof. What we saw was really shocking. There were hundreds of white handprints going around the flat roof, right up to the edge. The handprints were small but were human. It looked like the hands had been dipped in white paint. I looked closer, but it wasn't painted. It was almost like thick chalk.

My uncle told me not to mention it to anyone in the family, especially my grandmother. She had said all her life that Skinwalkers were after her. I didn't believe her, but after that night I began to wonder if she was telling the truth.

I later asked my uncle what he thought it was. He didn't hesitate and said it was witches. He said our family had been cursed during the old days before the treaties. He said someone in the family was a known witch, and when they were killed, the elders had placed a curse on the family. My uncle then laughed and said that no one outside of the family remembers any of that and it's probably a rumor anyway.

Well, it scared me enough that I believe that there may be something to that story. After that incident, I never spent another night at my grandmother's place again." JL

A Dewitt County, Texas, resident is walking around his town at night when he suddenly encounters a bizarre pale white crawling humanoid. He believes that the being is stalking him and causing a string of bad luck. This account was forwarded to me in August 2020:

"This encounter took place on January 12th, 2019, in Dewitt County, Texas. To be honest, I chose to go out on this night because my town was having a little ghost tour at the local haunted hospital. I was lonely and wanted to at least see others having fun.

It was 8 pm when I left the house and planned to be back within an hour. I have a routine of circling my town in the evening because I just like patrolling and there are always things creeping about after nightfall. I made my way to the haunted hospital, and once I got there, I saw flashlights inside the windows and heard laughter. Seeing others have fun made me smile and got rid of some of the loneliness I was feeling. This was the halfway point of my walk, and I started my second half heading home now.

There were some woods on the opposite side of town now but nothing impressive until I got to the last quarter of my walk. Now I was passing the baseball field on my left with a large wheat field on my right. This wheat field used to be a large extension of the woods but was cleared out for growing wheat. I continued again and crossed the small bridge that went over a creek and passed another section of woods. I was now headed towards an old metal building that has recently been turned into a place for making gates and fences. It was about 9 pm now.

This building had two small white houses beside it and a stretch of dirt road wrapping around the backside of it before returning to the normal asphalt road. Now at night, this place seems scary, but this was one of my favorite places to hang out at night and is a normal path I take my walks through.

As I was coming up to the dirt road, I saw a very tall 8-foot pale figure, with lanky arms almost dragging the ground, about 40 feet ahead of me, briskly walking from the white houses to the woods. I stopped walking. After a few minutes of standing there, I convinced myself to continue walking forward. I mean I was an adventurous person and there's no way I was just going to turn tail and go home when I just saw something so odd and out of place. Not even 15 seconds into walking forward this sudden heavy sense of dread overcame me like a giant weight crushing down on my shoulders. My instincts were telling me something was wrong.

I turned my iPhone light on and shined it in the woods. Nothing. I kept walking while keeping my head on a swivel, looking in all directions to keep my surroundings in check. About the fifth or sixth time I looked at the woods, I saw it. A huge bleached white humanoid figure crouched on all fours.

It was easily still 5–6 feet tall even though it was bent over. Its black eyes paralyzed me. It had a big round bald head and an extremely emaciated body, void of all hair, with very long almost dislocated-looking arms and legs. Its legs were like a flamingo bird at the knee as it bent backward instead of forward. I took all this in in a matter of seconds.

Suddenly it reminded me of a praying mantis when it swayed back and forth while staring as if deciding whether to attack or not. This broke me out of my trance, and I ran as fast as I could. I didn't look back until I had run a block. Out of breath and scared as heck, I finally took a glance back. I didn't see anything in sight. I didn't hear it chase me either. Maybe it was just stalking those people in those two little white houses and was waiting for me to go away to go back to its business. Maybe it didn't want anything to do with me. But that wasn't the end.

I got home, took a shower, and turned out the lights before I hopped in bed when suddenly there was something tapping on my window. 'Tap, tap, tap.' Three taps and nothing else. I lay in my bed that night wondering whether it had followed me home or not.

A string of bad luck ensued afterward the following weeks. I was constantly burning stuff on the stove that was relatively easy to make and I was an excellent cook on top of that. My dog started going nuts at night growling and barking at night in the living room and at the front door (which she has never ever done as she is the quietest sweetest dog you'll ever meet). And finally, I got deathly sick for three weeks straight with no sure sign of what I had. 103 fevers, vomiting with blood, sneezing, coughing, sore throat, migraines, nerve spasms, aching all over, etc. I've had smaller strings of bad luck before, after hearing its mimicry trying to lure me into the forest or seeing it one other time but I didn't see any details, but nothing ever this extreme. I don't go into the woods alone anymore." KN

Four friends are driving along an old road at night near Bay Minette in Baldwin County, Alabama, when they encounter a large pale quadruped humanoid standing in the middle of the road. A reader referred me to the following account in August 2020. I contacted the witness to confirm the incident:

"This incident took place in lower Alabama near Bay Minette when I was in high school, almost 8 years ago. But I still remember every detail. 3 friends and I were making the trip to our other friend's house, way out in the boondocks, probably 30 minutes outside of any nearby city or town. There's only one road that takes you to his house and it's just a long strip of old concrete that's in dire need of repair. But considering only a handful of people live out there, why would the state waste their time and money. On both sides of the road, it's just dense forest that creeps to the edge of the road sometimes (nowhere to pull off) and absolutely no streetlights.

We were in my friend's brand-new red Mustang that he got for his birthday, and he was proud to drive us all around wherever we wanted to go. Jamie was driving, my friend Dave in the passenger seat, and myself and my other friend Mary crammed in the backseat among his giant sound system (no seatbelts, just half standing, half sitting on the floorboards). It was very uncomfortable, and the rattling of the music shook my entire body, but I was just happy one of us had a vehicle to take us to our buddy's house.

We turned onto the long strip of road that would take us there and were very disappointed that there was another car not too far ahead of us, which meant Jamie couldn't show off how fast his new car could go. Although there are no crazy turns/curves in the road, it's a solid white line the whole way because of the endless hills, making it impossible to pass anyone. We accepted that we'd have to go the speed limit and Jamie finally turned the music down so he could talk about the tiny red Toyota that we'd be staring at the back of for a while.

It's about 9 PM and there was no moon visible through the dense clouds, so it was pitch black besides our headlights and the car in front of us with its own lights. No other vehicles came from the other direction, and no one was behind us. We drove for only about 10 minutes, cutting up and hardly paying attention to the road since we knew where we were going.

Suddenly, the car in front of us slams on its brakes, skidding its tires, stopping in the middle of the road. Jamie wasn't following too closely so we didn't have to do the same, but we came to a slow stop maybe 15 feet behind them. There was a brief pause before we heard a woman's blood-curdling scream coming from the Toyota (we had the windows down because some of us had been smoking) and that's when we saw it.

We had stopped on a declining hill so we could see in front of the Toyota, and what we saw, I'll never be able to forget. It was [a] humanoid-looking creature, standing on all fours, but the arch of its back was taller than the little Toyota. The only thing that made it 'humanoid' was its hairless skin, but it was very pale, almost grey, very wrinkly, and its limbs were impossibly long (its forearm was longer than any human's entire arm). The legs, fingers, arms, neck, everything looked like stretched taffy and we could see all its bones through its skin, especially the backbones that were almost spike-like because they jutted out so much. It wasn't facing us, just stopped mid-stride in the middle of the road, facing the right side of the forest. It had backward-facing knees like a bird's legs, no tail, but still had the posture of an animal. I hoped to God it was an animal, but there's no animal in Alabama that would be taller than a car on all fours, and as I said, it had human-like skin, hands, feet, and its head was like a human skull.

"No one in our car said a word and Jamie instinctively hit the lock button for the doors, though our windows were still down, and the woman in the Toyota was still screaming bloody murder.

For a moment, I remember telling myself it was just some kind of prank or a weird art sculpture because it wasn't moving at all. But then those thoughts quickly dissipated when the thing cocked its head in our direction. Its face was just as terrible as the rest of its body, pale and wrinkly, just an indention for a nose, tiny black holes for eyes, no ears, and an impossibly large, red-stained mouth that formed into a wicked smile, showing its multiple rows of pointed teeth. The woman's scream grew terribly louder at that moment and the thing seemed to finally be almost startled by it, turning its head back towards the forest, taking only about 2 giant, fluid, animal-like steps, and disappearing into the woods on our right without any sound.

As soon as it was out of sight, Jamie slowly crept the Mustang forward, around the still-stopped Toyota and we saw a man and woman frantically arguing and crying in the front seats. When we got in front of them, the man puts the Toyota in reverse and goes a bit off-road to turn around, and floors it in the direction we came from. Apparently, where they were headed wasn't important enough. I almost thought we should do the same, but I couldn't get myself to make a sound, let alone a word or sentence. Jamie went only about 5 miles over the speed limit as he rolled the windows up and no one said a word for the rest of the 20-minute drive.

When we finally got to our friend's house, he was waiting outside for us, waving as we pulled in the little dirt driveway. All four of us scrambled out, pushing past him to get inside the house. I remember him saying something like, 'Woah, looks like you guys saw a ghost or something!' Dave turns to him with the most serious face and says, 'Or something. Yeah.'

We got inside and part of me was still thinking it was some sort of hallucination. I was the artist of the group, so I asked our friend for paper and pencils. Without question, he retrieved them, and while sitting in his living room, I suggested that we all should try to draw exactly what we saw before we tried to discuss anything. Sure enough, each of us drew the exact same creature and showed it to our friend before explaining the full story. He was horrified and took the drawings out back to his small fire pit and lit them ablaze. None of us protested because we never wanted a visual of that thing again. He asked us things like had we been drugged or were we pulling a fast one on him. But considering there were two other people that saw the same thing and most of us were to the point of tears, he knew we weren't lying. He led us back inside, locked his doors and windows, and put on a movie to distract us. But we kept bringing it up, trying to make any sense out of it.

Jamie took us all home the next day and we saw the Toyota's black skid marks in the road where it happened, confirming it wasn't all an elaborate shared dream. Before we dropped off Mary, she told us she didn't want to hang out with us anymore, simply because being around us would remind her of it. We sort of just nodded, and I honestly haven't spoken to her since. I rarely speak to the other 2 friends anymore, for other reasons, but a few times I've tried to bring it up to them, and they refuse to talk about it. I know they know it happened, it's just too painful for them to discuss, which is understandable. I hate talking about it to this day and have only told 2 of my closest friends and my now boyfriend who's very opposed to any 'supernatural' things. So, you can understand why I didn't get any relief by talking to him about it.

I never really believed in those sorts of things either before that incident, but it's changed my perspective a bit. Please let me know if any of you have seen something similar. I've tried researching it, and I guess I'd just like to put a name to whatever that terrible thing that prowls [the] lower Alabama woods was." TD

Two young Navajo men in New Mexico are out late at night in a nearby canyon when they encounter a tall misshapen humanoid that was walking ahead of them and mumbling. This account was told to me by the late crypto-investigator Jc Johnson:

"This happened to my older brother, who we can call 'Danny.' It was back in the early 2000s and he was a senior in high school in a small podunk New Mexico town. Being a senior and a football player, he was kind of an idiot and did stupid things, one of which included walking through the woods late at night, as he called it, 'throw rocks and terrorize kids from school.' Yes, immature, I know, but he and his accomplice (another Navajo called 'Joe') were seniors and on the football team. They walked through the woods because cops patrolled the streets, and there was a city curfew in place. The route they took went through a state park which has lots of Navajo artifacts and even a kiva which you can go down into.

So, one night they were sneaking through the forest before the sun had risen, and they had begun to stop and shush each other because they could sometimes hear footsteps in the distance. Unless some other geniuses had the idea to walk through the desert, there should have been no one else out there. This continued for a while, until Joe stopped Danny, grabbed him, and said, 'Get down!'

They dropped to their stomachs and hid, listening. Now the footsteps, crunching through the desert foliage, were accompanied by mumbling. Danny estimated that the sounds were maybe 100 feet away at first but got closer. He doesn't know if the mutterings were Navajo or English or some other language. After a while of the noises staying far away, Joe whispered without looking, 'It sounds like a drunk.' Several more minutes and Danny decided to chance a peek, as the 'drunk' sounded more distant now.

It was night, but the moon was bright, and the light bounced off the canyon wall nearby. Danny was looking for a man, but instead, he saw a figure which he said, 'moved with a tilt to its body' and was 'long and tall.' It was human-formed and walking on two feet, but misshapen and VERY tall. He said it resembled a Kokopelli or Navajo kachina doll, so not exactly normal shaped. It mumbled and drifted through the trees seemingly looking for something. He was captivated, watching it for a few minutes, and then suddenly the snapping twigs and the mutterings just stopped. Everything was quiet. And the figure, whatever it was, had just disappeared.

After that, Danny and Joe both 'felt' that whatever was in the forest at the time was gone. They sat on the ground afterward discussing what had just happened. Joe asked about what Danny had seen, and then stated, 'I didn't look because if I would have, it would have known we were both staring.'

I forgot to ask him if he and Joe went back through the

woods, but the answer is probably yes. This kind of happening is pretty common within the Navajo culture and it's something they're used to dealing with." Name withheld.

I received the next account in November 2020:

"This past winter, my wife and I decided to make the drive to Colorado Springs on the recommendation of a friend of mine. She'd never seen mountains before, so I figured the Rockies would be perfect. We stayed in a Holiday Inn that was right at the base of the mountain basically and had a great view of Pikes Peak as soon as we looked out the window. She was thrilled, she had never seen anything like it before, and she's a sucker for a gift shop, so this place was great. We had a great time.

On our second day there we decided to drive up to Pikes Peak, but we were told at the gate we could go up most of the way, but the very summit was closed off because there was too much snow. We could still get far up though. I think Pikes Peak is around 14,000 feet, and we got to like 11,000 feet before it was closed off. So, we were up above the awesome clouds because it just looked like looking out over the ocean. We stopped at the little rest center on the way up to get hot chocolate for the drive and a magnet for Colorado since we collect magnets for every state we go to.

It was cool because there were 'Bigfoot Crossing' signs along the way up, which was fun to take a picture in front of. Anyway, once we got to the closed-off part of Pikes Peak, we parked our car and got out and just kind of took in the view. I didn't think anybody else was up there with us, except the guy a little up the way sitting in his truck making sure people didn't go up any higher than they were supposed to. Even if we couldn't go to the summit, it was still gorgeous. I wandered off and started looking around the rocks and what few trees were up at that elevation. I just like to explore stuff off the beaten path.

I heard some snow crunching nearby and assumed it was another sightseer, so I moved toward the sound of the crunching snow but didn't see anybody. There are a few trees here and there but not hard to see. It was snowing a bit, however, and the wind was blowing the snow sideways. I'd gone far from my wife at this point and didn't want to stray too much farther, but I was honestly hoping to see a wolf or something. I found tracks in the snow, and they were small.

I did not see a wolf. At first, I didn't see anything. I followed the tracks around a tree and kind of carefully peeked around it but didn't see anything. The tracks stopped there, though. I didn't get right up on the tree because if it was a wolf I mean, I didn't want to get face to face with it.

What I did see, eventually, was a pure white 'thing' scurrying away from the exact location I was looking. It was pure white. I'm not sure if it was invisible, or just blended in perfectly with the snow. It moved on all fours, had a huge bulbous head, kind of like the way you think of the typical version of an alien, and it had a spindly body. Its arms and legs were super skinny, and its body wasn't a whole lot bigger. Its arms and legs themselves were long. I'd say it was probably between 4-5 feet tall if it were standing upright. It was a bit hard to tell with it always on all fours, and in the snow. It turned around and looked at me, and had small, black eyes, and no defining features. Its eyes were far apart and almost on the side of its head. Its feet and hands were buried but when it went to move, I saw what its hand looked like. It had fingers that were way too long. Like, not ET long, but wiry, spindly fingers. It looked at me for just a second and then leaped forward away from me and as soon as it landed in the snow it was invisible again, or I just couldn't see it. Then it hopped again (and it jumped a good 6 feet or so from a dead stop) and took off running. It ran away from me and scaled some rocks in the distance like it was nothing and crawled along the cliffside. Whenever it was in the snow it looked invisible though. I'm not sure if that's because it was all white, or because it was like, turning invisible. Anyway, in a few seconds it was gone.

When I got back to my wife, who was waiting in the car, she didn't believe a word of it and thought I was just trying to scare her. To this day she doesn't believe me. And I don't what it was. I've never heard of any cryptid or anything like it, and on the trek back down I asked the lady at the gift shop if people ever reported seeing weird things and she just mentioned Bigfoot." DL

A college student, living at home, recounts the strange activity occurring in and around her family's home. Her brother states that he had two encounters with a pale humanoid in the yard. I received this account in December 2020:

"I have no clue what is going on. I live in north-central Massachusetts in Middlesex County, in the middle of the woods. We're a few miles out of town. For the past few months, my family and I have become convinced our house is haunted, but I wasn't bothered by it. Whatever it is isn't too much of a nuisance and hasn't done anything to harm us, so we don't mind. It has mostly just been apparitions, things turning on their own, and our pets getting spooked by nothing. That was until the more physical things started to happen, and I'm not sure if they are somehow connected to the peaceful presence in our house.

About a month ago I was up late around 3 am watching

YouTube. It was warm out, so I had my window open along with the curtain. Suddenly, I heard what sounded like a grown man angrily scream right in our yard. My heart dropped and I was frozen in fear. Like I said before, we're in the middle of the woods and there are only a few houses around us; no one would be screaming in our yard at 3 am. I lay there for a few minutes listening for anything else, and I even renewed the video I was watching to make sure what I heard wasn't just in the video.

Finally, I got the courage to get up. I closed my window and woke up my mom, who I still live with. She went around the house with me, turning on all the outside lights and seeing if there was anyone in our yard. There was nothing. I keep thinking about how if I hadn't lain there paralyzed with fear, I would've been able to see whoever or whatever it was.

The next night I slept with my window open again and I had the most vivid dream I have ever had. In it, I was watching myself sleep, but outside the window staring in at me was the extremely pale face. It looked almost human, but not quite. I ended up jolting awake completely terrified, and slamming my window shut and closing the shade. But I just kept having the dream repeatedly for the next few days.

Over the next few weeks, I kept hearing weird noises in the woods in broad daylight as well as late at night. It sounded like something was hitting branches with a stick. Even my dog heard it and was running around the yard barking up a storm to defend his house.

Fast forward to yesterday, my brother was home alone around 9 pm. He went to let our dog outside, but when he got out onto our indoor porch, he saw something in the yard. The only light in the backyard was coming from the light inside the house. It illuminated a tall humanoid figure (maybe around 7 feet tall) in the yard, standing about fifteen feet away from the house, right in front of our fire pit. It had no clothes on, was incredibly skinny, and it was so pale that it appeared to glow in the light. Thankfully, he did not let our dog out and went inside locking the doors and shutting the windows, waiting for our mom to get home.

I know that he could just be lying, but when our mom got home, he was terrified, and just hid in the living room until she got there. I've known him his whole life and he has never lied about something like this and is a horrible liar. So, I'm confident he is telling the truth.

I'm currently sitting out on my indoor porch at around 8 pm typing this, waiting to see if I can spot it or at least hear something. I'm honestly debating on whether I should sleep out here.

I did a little reading beforehand on some creatures and came across the mention of crawlers. When my brother described it, he said it was standing completely upright; he didn't see it walk or crawl in any way. Could it still be a crawler? Are we in any danger? And is it possible that it is somehow connected to the paranormal stuff that has been happening in our house?" MB

UPDATE: "About 3 or 4 days after my original email, my brother saw the creature again. I was home, but I was in the middle of a long nap in my room, so it was just my brother and my mom. It was probably around 8 pm and my mom was in the living room on the phone and my brother was just watching TV beside her. Our dog was outside and started barking at something, and keep in mind that he always does this. He'll bark at any living creature he sees on our property or walking in front of the house on the road, so neither of them thought anything about it. My brother got up to let him in and walked onto our indoor porch and looked out to see what our dog was barking at. He saw the creature again, about ten feet from where he saw it originally, staring at the house again. He ran back to the living room to get our mom, who came out to look. By the time they got to the porch, the creature was just gone.

I'm just not convinced something is going on after my brother saw it the second time. He started saying that he's scared; he's just hallucinating, and his mind or eyes were just playing tricks on him. Especially since when he got my mom, the creature had disappeared within those fifteen-seconds without even the smallest trace. So, because he was starting to be convinced it was just a trick his eyes played on him, I stop believing that he saw a crawler. I just kind of stopped caring.

My one class for yesterday was canceled, so I spent the whole day just lounging around. I completely forgot about making myself dinner, so it was about 11:45 pm when I remembered. I was just quickly making some chili when my mom got up to let my dog outside. It had been down pouring all day, so my dog had only gone outside twice during the day because he's terrified of rain. My mom went back to bed and left me to let him in when he's done.

I finished making my dinner about ten minutes later and decided to go call him to have him come back inside. Once I called him, I heard something big move in the woods as if it reacted to my voice. Immediately after that, my dog came charging from the other side of the yard and proceeded to freak out over whatever was hidden in the trees. I kept calling him, but he would not stop barking and growling no matter what. I even shouted out some of his favorite phrases, but he didn't react to any of them at all which was super strange because he always does, no matter how distracted he is. This went on for a few minutes and it got to the point where my mom and my sister came out so we could all try to call him back inside. We didn't want him to wake up the entire neighborhood.

Now, I don't know if I'm brave, or just literally the stupidest person alive, but I decided to just go out into our woodsy backyard (barefoot) in the middle of the night to force him to come inside. It was about 40 degrees F, and I was only wearing a sports bra and shorts; I was angry and just wanted to eat my food. I went outside and walked down the steps from the indoor porch, and I was about ten feet into the yard when I heard whatever it was moving in the woods again in response to me walking into the yard. I froze for a few seconds, and I heard my sister from above me on the porch go, 'WTF was that?' I didn't care when I heard it move when I was on the porch but hearing it maybe not even thirty feet from me when there aren't any walls around me, scared the crap out of me.

Regardless, I started walking again towards my dog to put his leash on him, but as soon as he saw the leash in my hand, he ran back to the porch, leaving me alone in the dark. I have never run faster in my life. I got back to the porch, let my dog in, everyone went back to bed, and I finally ate my chili (the only good part of this story).

Now, I know there's no guarantee that it was whatever my brother saw or thinks he saw, after all, I'm still not fully convinced it even exists, but the entire situation was very strange. We live in the middle of the woods; we're used to wildlife being around our house and my dog always barks at any living thing he sees or hears near the house. However, every single time he barks at them, we always hear them running away in the woods to get away from him. From tiny bunnies to a bear, it's always the same. But whatever was in the woods tonight obviously did not care about my dog barking and growling and charging around the yard. It just seemed to move around anytime something new happened, like me calling for my dog or me going out into the yard. It seemed like it was just watching.

Also, my dog has a very specific bark. It can be annoying as hell, but it's always the same. Whenever he sees or hears something near or on our property it's almost as if he's yelling, 'Hey! Get out of here!' But he doesn't sound angry at all. I've even seen him charge at a full-grown male deer three times his size, and his bark was just the same old 'get off my lawn!' But tonight, when he was barking at whatever was in the woods, he sounded so angry and vicious. I don't think I've ever heard him bark or growl like that. I was shocked.

Anyways that's it. That happened exactly 24 hours ago now. As for the paranormal stuff in my house that I mentioned in the original email, it's been about the same. Just small things have been happening along with knocks on walls. Any thoughts?" MB

This next account was received in May 2021:

"I want to share an experience I had while training with my National Guard unit at Fort McCoy, Wisconsin. I moved from enlisted to the officer via ROTC and was attached to a unit in my prospective MOS while in the program. I don't really want to give specifics on my service, as the community is small enough to identify me to peers.

In 2014 my platoon decided to conduct nighttime land navigation at Fort McCoy from 2030 to 0030. While the Army is typically all about buddy pairs, night land navigation is one of the few cases we can do things solo if we so choose. Having done night land navigation plenty before, I step off alone, compass, map, and headlamp in hand.

For those who do not know; land navigation involves

seeking out markers on a course by plotting their coordinates on a map and moving there via terrain reference and compass. At night this is typically done without light as much as possible. When light is used it is red. This minimizes damage to night vision. Ostensibly, these methods also keep you concealed in a tactical environment when employed with noise discipline.

I bring this up so you can understand a few things about my circumstance. I was moving through the woods while making a token effort to be hard to spot/hear. The woodland I was in was part of a larger forest system but was frequently traveled. That night we had some 15 soldiers clomping around. My illumination was a togglable headlamp but was toggled to be red when turned on. To cycle to white light, I must turn it off twice (the cycle was off – solid white – off – flashing white – off – solid red – off – flashing red – off – solid white).

My assigned points will take me to the other side of the course and back. A good hour and a half of walking as the crow flies. They're in a straight line so I estimate two and a half hours out and back. I know if I come back too early, I might be given another set of points. So, I resolve to walk out, take a break for an hour then mosey on back.

The first half of this goes as planned, I get my points without much trouble and wind up sitting on a hillside at around 10 at night. It's cloudy, but the moon is full. I can see well when the sky is clear, poorly when it's not. Occasionally, I see a red light bobbing in the distance below me. Once a pair of platoon members pass down the hill from me, using white light to try to read their map. I startle them when I ask if they needed help.

At the end of my break, there's no more motion in my area. Most people had likely already walked out and back, or they were too lost and took the handrailing road home. I'm feeling pretty at one with my surroundings, having sat in the same spot eating stale Skittles for a good long while. Owls hoot, trees sway, all is well.

I trot down my hill and step through some brush. I'm in a clearing where prairie intersects forest. There are some dead trees in the area, one of them is split halfway up. At the top (15 feet) I can make out a head and shoulders silhouetted against the clouds backlit by the moon. I walk up to ask how they got up there (and if they're stuck) when the shadow twitches and I get the impression it's turned toward me. I stand there looking at it, and it's maybe looking at me.

The situation feels off, but I'm not going to let a battle buddy punk me. I ask if they need a hand. Midsentence, the moonlight comes back. It's clear the thing on the tall stump is not a soldier.

This moonlight glimpse is the best look I get at the thing. It looks like a stretched-out bald person. Its long arms are clutching the stump. I can't make out the face, but it looks pinched. By that I mean I couldn't see its eyes or mouth like they were small and in the middle of the head. It's skinny like it hasn't eaten, but it's tall and obviously strong to have made such a vertical climb.

It was facing me. It probably was the whole time I was in the clearing. Maybe since I came down the hill. Maybe my speech startled it.

I swear loudly. It rapidly scurries down the trunk. I flick on my red light and catch it on all fours moving toward the brush line in the direction I'm heading. Automatically, I keep toggling the lamp to be in white light. That means it goes off, then to flashing red. In the flash, I see the thing at the wood line, but I think it's flipped around and is backing in (probably to keep eyes on me). In the few seconds it takes for me to get to white light it's gone.

I scan the tree line which is silent. When it moved there was a scraping noise, plus the woodland brush is dense. If it was still running, I would hear it. I reason that it must have stopped. It must still be watching me. I fumble out my knife and keep looking around the woods in front of me. After ages, I start inching along a perpendicular path to my initial route of travel, an angle that will link me up with the hardball road that runs up and down the side of the course. Once on the road, I can take it back to where my platoon is parked.

My major problem is that the road is ten minutes of walking away from my current position, mostly woodland. That can't be helped, I have to get out of the clearing first. My progress on that front is painfully slow. I'm fighting my natural urge to freeze in place like a deer in the headlights.

After sidestepping a good 10 meters I hear a corresponding rustling and think I see movement. It's enough to get me to turn and bolt, right into a downed log that trips me. I scramble up to my feet and look back to the wood line where there is an audible commotion. I glimpse a leg and ass moving back into the woods. At this point, I'm done with the whole situation, but don't want to run again. I start power walking to the road, turning to look as much as I can while seeing what the thing is doing.

Over the movement of my own kit, I can hear it moving alongside me, parallel. As I near the end of the clearing I think I hear it picking up pace as if to cut me off. I make the decision to sprint. When I enter the woods, my path is clear, but I think I can hear it in my periphery. I don't stop and run hard until I hit the paved road. I bite it hard a few times along the way but recover with a frantic speed I cannot consciously replicate.

Once in the road, I run perpendicular to the forest until I don't think I hear it anymore. I'm winded from my break-out run. From the middle of the road [I] have good visibility and decide to walk to catch my breath.

It's quiet for a while. Then I hear a branch move around thirty feet in the air from the woods I had just fled. I snap my gaze up, see a pale ovular face, half in shadow peeking at me from around a trunk. I take off again. After way too long I make it back to the headlights of our LMTVs. It's 1215.

'What happened, cadet, did you get lost out there?' 'You're covered in mud. Did you fall down?' 'Why are you out of breath?'

'I got lost on my way back.'

I knew better than to claim I saw a monster. Already my reaction had left me feeling foolish.

"In the years since drilling at FMC, I have never experienced anything like that again. McCoy does not have a history of disappearances, as far as I know, neither do the two closest towns (Sparta and Tomah). I've done night land navigation alone a few times since without issue. This is less from courage, and more from me deciding I must have misinterpreted the situation. Maybe the world is weirder than I thought." R

A couple in Monterey, California, is driving late at night along a dark winding road when the woman glimpses a bizarre humanoid figure and panics. What did she see? This report was submitted to me in May 2021:

"This happened to me while I was in college (20+ years ago), and I never forgot it. It was one of the first times I ever remember seeing true fear and panic on someone's face.

This part will only spatially make sense if you are

familiar with Monterey, California. I lived in the Seaside area, and my college girlfriend lived in Carmel Valley. Sometimes when I would drive her home late at night, we would take a lightly used roadway called Laureles Grade. It was long, dark, and full of winding turns. It also let us out near her house, so it was a minor time saver.

We were driving home late one night, and we were chatting and laughing about something or another, as we usually did on the ride. Then she looks out the window, stops mid-sentence, SCREAMS, then looks forward and yells GO! She is terrified at this point! I floor it and ask her what is happening, and she won't talk. She is next to me hyperventilating.

I drove unsafely fast through the twists and turns of the road and a few minutes later slowed down if whatever scared her was fast in our rearview. By this point, she is calmed a bit as well and I ask her again what happened.

Her first reply was, 'You didn't see it?' She then proceeds to tell me that as we were driving around a corner, she was looking out the window and my headlights lit up a human-looking animal, standing along the side of the road disjointedly on all fours, with a human-like face that looked like it was hissing.

My first reaction was that it might be a hurt person and maybe we should go back or call 911, but she was adamant that 'NO, it was NOT a person, and there was no way we're going back!'

We got to her house a few minutes later and, out of extra precaution, called the local police and asked them to go and check the area. We never had any follow-up from them.

Fast forward several years (15 or so) and I was telling a coworker who was from that area about the incident. She got spooked and when I finished, she told me that Laureles Grade was known for strange sightings and is a spot that

UFO fanatics tend to go to (I'm NOT a UFO guy) which I thought was interesting." HF

An Alexandria, Virginia, witness encountered a small-bodied humanoid with short white hair, a bulbous head, and long lanky appendages. Was it a crawler, or something entirely different? This account was forwarded to me in May 2021:

"This happened one night in Alexandria, Virginia, about 4 years ago. I don't live there anymore so I don't care about specific locations here. Also, there is no history of mental illness in my family, and I've never had any issues with hallucinations.

Anyway, one night I decided to drive up to the 7-11 for an apple fritter. It was 2:30 am and I was wide awake. My toxic relationship had just ended like 2 minutes prior, so I was kind of stoked. So, I hop in my car and when I get out to the main road it was dead. I was the only person on the road at that time on Franconia Rd., for those interested. I drove onto the left turn lane to go down a little side street that took you behind the 7-11.

As I'm starting to cross the oncoming lanes, I noticed some weird shape moving next to my driver's side door. So, I stop and look out my window and I got a good look at this thing. It was trotting (the only word I can think to describe it) on all fours. Its body was about as big as a one-year-old baby's, but its arms and legs were long and skinny (like maybe 2.5 to 3 ft. long). It had a bulbous head on a skinny neck and was covered with white hair that looked short and bristly. The thing that got me is the fact it had hands and feet.

So, it continues to trot diagonally across the intersection until it gets in my headlight beams and when it does it takes off fast as hell. Its stride was so long, and it covered so much ground in such a short time. It got at least 50 yards away from me and jumped into some bushes next to the palm reader behind the BP station. I have no idea what it could be. Has anyone else in the DMV area seen anything like this?" XC

The District of Columbia suburbs of Northern Virginia have been a hotspot for unexplained humanoid activity in recent years. There is no evidence or explanation as to why this is occurring.

A northern Wisconsin teen is with her boyfriend when she begins to experience panic attacks along a certain country road. Later, she observes several small hairless humanoid creatures along the same road. This strange incident was reported in May 2021:

"This happened to me yesterday (Monday, May 3rd) and I am still processing it. To preface, I live in northern Wisconsin in an area that has a large Ojibwa population. One thing I have learned from living here is if a native tells you something is wrong, you listen to them. They've been here longer than us and they know what's going on. I'm a 16-year-old female and a junior in high school. Last night was my junior prom and I went with my boyfriend.

Because of Covid, the prom was hosted by parents a couple of towns over at a town hall. We had to drive, and my boyfriend picked me up. The highway that leads to this town is desolate and runs straight through a forest. It's about 15 miles long.

This would be fine, but then we entered this specific area on the highway. I'm a level-headed person. I don't scare easily. When we entered this area, I felt nothing but pure terror. We were surrounded by nothing but woods and I felt like I was being hunted. There were these garbage bags on the side of the road. The first garbage bag was on the left side of the road. I pointed it out to my boyfriend, and he said that someone probably dumped it there so they wouldn't have to pay for garbage pickup. I believe him until we came upon two more garbage bags a couple of miles down the road. They were on opposite sides of the road, equal lengths apart. I shrugged it off. Then equal distances away there were two more garbage bags. This continued for the remainder of the stretch of the road until the end, where there was a single garbage bag, now on the right.

I told my boyfriend that the road was giving me a weird vibe and he did his best to calm my anxieties. He thought I was worried because the road had a fast speed limit (65–70 mph), but it wasn't fear like that. It was primal fear. Something there above me on the food chain.

Everything was fine until we left the dance. When pulling out of the parking lot, we saw a cop. The cop pulled onto the highway leading to this road when they saw us coming. They didn't use a turn signal, which was very illegal. The cop started acting very weird. While in front of us, they were swerving and kept hugging the line. Then right before we reached the road, the cop with NO warning I may add, just stopped, did a U-turn not even 50 feet from our car, and hauled ass off the road. No sirens, no lights, not even a turn signal. My boyfriend and I were weirded out. It didn't help that this road was pitch black and the only light was his car's crappy high beams.

We then entered the road. And again, I was terrified. After passing the first garbage bag, the sense of primal fear returned. I wanted out. I started shaking and crying and my boyfriend did his very best to comfort me. He suggested pulling over until I calmed down but I refused. At that moment, I was sure that if we pulled over, we would die. I just kept repeating the phrase 'Something's not right here.' He stepped on the gas.

Being 9:30–10 at night, we were the only ones on this road. Off in the distance behind us, we saw a glowing pair of LED high beam lights. They were pulling up on us fast. Might I keep you in mind, the speed limit here was 65–70, this car was going at least 85–90. And this driver was none other than the cop from before. This cop, again, no sirens or lights, sped right past us and off into the distance. Something in my gut told me that whoever was in that car was feeling the same way I was.

Nothing changed for a bit. My boyfriend talked me down and I was calm. But then suddenly, I felt the terror again. It was stronger than ever. I started having a panic attack and screaming. I was crying and begging my boyfriend to leave because something was wrong. Then I looked out my window and saw them. There were 5–10 little creatures coming out of the woods. One looked me right in the eyes and I knew this thing was a predator.

They were a bit larger than a raccoon and walked on all fours. Completely hairless. They looked humanoid and wrinkled. Imagine the top half of the Fuji mermaid, but larger and not dried out. Another way to describe them is a smaller version of the rake. They had eyes that reflected light or that glowed in the dark. They were skinny and frail looking.

I scream and beg my boyfriend to keep driving. He obliged and did. Eventually, we left that road and got back to a more populated area of the highway. He pulled over and began to comfort me. I was having a panic attack. I tried to tell him what I saw but I just couldn't. I told him I saw a malformed raccoon. He just laughed it off.

We returned to my house, and I was terrified. I had explained to my mother that something was wrong with that road. She shrugged it off but allowed my boyfriend to stay the night, which made me feel better that he didn't have to leave and got to stay at my house, away from the woods and those things. My dad, whom we told about the cop, said that the cop was just trying to rouse us. That the cop was hoping we'd make a mistake, and they could ticket us. I'm not sure if that's true.

I called my best friend today. She is Ojibwa, who practices the beliefs and culture. When we were talking, I couldn't help but spill. I told her about the creatures in the woods, and the cop, and the trash bags. She sounded worried. She said the trash bags were most likely from people who volunteer to clean highways, which I can agree with. They were clear bags; I could see trash in them. She was worried about the creatures. She started asking me questions. She asked if I was on my period. She asked about the spiritual healing practice my mother takes me to. She asked if I tried to contact a spirit or if I tried to play with something dead. I told her about the natural healing (my mother has me doing NAET for my allergies) and that I hadn't tried to play with the dead. I told her that that day was the day after my period had just finished.

She told me in a concerned voice that the NAET may have opened my third eye and that those creatures may have been attracted to me because of my period. She told me that she was going to give me sage and that I needed to use it. She asked me to redraw what I saw, and I did. I sent the picture to her, and she said that it was weird, but that I should be safe. I am still shaken up. Those things wanted me and were out for blood. I don't think I'll ever go back there again." SH

The following account was forwarded to me in June 2021:

"The summer after graduating high school in the metro Detroit area of Michigan, almost every weekend was grad party after grad party. Towards the end of the summer, one of my closest friends had his at his house. Now, his house backs up to a small, wooded area, probably no more than 50–100 yards deep and maybe 20–30 yards across. It's small enough to where you can see the house on the other side of it during the day and some of the lights on in that house at night. Additionally, the houses surrounding him belong primarily to the elderly, so no one is out past 10 o'clock or so. Finally, we had never drunk or tried any sort of intoxicating substance until months after this all occurred. This all comes into play as the night begins to unfold.

Once it started to get dark out, the party died off. At this point, it was only me, him, and three of our friends. Around 10:00 PM we thought it would be a good night for a bonfire, so we got some wood together, along with the lighter fluid and lighter, and got a nice little fire going. We spent a good hour or so just having a good time, sharing stories, and laughing until one of our friends had to leave. This left only four of us until about half an hour later when one of our other friends had to leave. So, her boyfriend took her home and told us he'd be back in a little bit. Suddenly it was the two of us.

This is when things got interesting.

As my friend sat facing back towards the woods, and I with my back to the woods, we started hearing some noises. Sticks cracking on the ground, and leaves being brushed through, those sorts of things. He laughed it off saying it was just the neighbor's cat. As we sat and continued to shoot the sh*t, the noises continued, and I continued to brush them off under the assumption it was just a cat. However, I was a little unnerved when we both heard what sounded like footsteps in the front yard. At first, we thought our friend had gotten back but realized it wasn't him after a few minutes had gone by. Eventually, our friend came back from dropping his girlfriend off at home and we started talking again like nothing had ever happened.

A couple of minutes later, however, the noises from the woods started up again, but this time they were closer. Much closer. I could see my friend was unnerved by this and I reminded him he told me it was just the cat. He looked at me and told me that they didn't have a cat, he just said that to reassure himself earlier that it was nothing. I quickly got up, moved to the other side of the fire, and sat down between my two friends so that we were all facing the woods. After using a few choice words towards my friend to express how I felt about him letting me sit with my back towards whatever was back there, things took a bit of a turn.

We saw something move in the brush. It was slight but noticeable. It looked big too, about five feet tall. Kind of human-like. We tried to joke it off and convince ourselves it was nothing. This worked until a few moments later when we started to see more movement. This continued for a couple of minutes until it got significantly closer, and we decided to go inside. We hurried as we started to grab everything we needed to take in and put the lid on the fire pit (just an old dome-shaped metal BBQ grill without the legs).

Throughout this time, it continued to move closer to us. It almost seemed hesitant yet curious as we saw it dart about. Nonetheless, we rushed inside. We locked the door behind us and went to the windows. By this point, it knew we were inside and was coming up to the house. It would dart by the windows as we ran between the windows in the house in hopes we could catch a glimpse of what had us so scared. We made out some basic details. It was about 4 to 5 feet tall when it was hunched over, humanoid, and pale. Almost white but still a little gray kind of pale. This lasted for a good ten minutes until we heard the scratching of nails on the wooden deck connected to the house.

Around this time, it seemed to shift its focus towards the fire as we didn't put the lid back on completely. Before I knew it, my friend was calling us over to the window that faced the fire. The lid was off, and we could see the shape of it darting around the fire. We later found the lid about 10 feet away from the pit. Something had to have picked it up by the hot metal handle and thrown it over there. Around this time, we also noticed that it was around some of the other windows. It was then that we realized there wasn't just one of whatever it was. There were multiples. If I had to guess, I'd say there were about 4 or 5.

This general activity continued for about 20 minutes until I decided I was going home. Our other friend decided he would do the same at that point so neither of us would have to walk to our cars alone. We both parked maybe 20–30 yards from the house but since the activity had only increased since it started, 20 yards seemed like a mile because of our nerves. After our friend tried and failed to convince us to stay the night there with him, we left. Out the front door and to our cars within about 30 seconds. As we went to get in our cars, however, we faced the backyard, and both saw multiple of the things crouched down about halfway to the ground. Some in open parts of the yard looking at us and some behind the trees looking back at the house.

As we both drove away, I looked back and saw the shape of a head looking into one of the windows of the house. As we left his neighborhood (which is kind of hidden in a wooded area) we both saw something cross the street behind our cars. As soon as we both got back to our houses, we got onto our group chat to confirm what we saw after leaving the house.

Any doubt I had about what I saw was quickly thrown out the window as soon as my friend described what he saw without any input as to what I saw.

As the three of us recounted the night in our group chat, my friend continued to update us on the events still unfolding at his house. Besides seeing the figures outside his window still, he claimed he saw a face in the window at one point. Pale skin and black eyes. He described them as almost being like holes in the face they were so dark. He also claimed at one point something had scratched the screen on his window.

We were all terrified, to say the least. Any sensible person wouldn't try to recreate the events from that night, right? Well, I guess we're not the most sensible people because the next night we were right back at it. We knew what we saw, and we needed validation. This time we had another person stay with us so they could back up our claims. We needed evidence that was better than just our word. It was too dark to take pictures or video.

We set the night up just like the previous. Everyone got to the house, we got a nice fire going, and we waited for things to start up. Once it got dark out, we started hearing the rustling in the brush again. An hour or so later the noises got closer, and I switched sides so that all four of us were facing the wooded area. Within minutes, we saw whatever was out there moving through the brush again. There were probably about two or three at this point. We tried to hold out for a while, thinking we were hot sh*t, and it wouldn't come for us.

This attitude changed within a matter of minutes as the pale figures got closer and started to go to the sides of us. They were surrounding us. We got up and calmly tried to put the lid back on the fire. We figured if we showed we were afraid, they might go for us. As soon as we finished getting the lid on the fire and grabbed everything we needed, we rushed inside. Before we knew it, they were darting past the windows again. At this point, the fourth person, who hadn't been with us during it all the night before, agreed that something was out there.

As time passed, we gathered up the courage to go back out and stand on the deck and try to get evidence. We stood out there as they got closer. There was more this time. Maybe five or six. We stood there in silence as we observed them. They almost seemed curious with a hint of mischief. Some watched us, some ran around. One even scratched the underside of the deck directly beneath my feet. I could feel it as its nail dragged across the wood. At one point a deer ran out of the wooded area just a bit further down the road. It was like it was running away from something, but not us because it ran somewhat towards us. Not away from us.

Throughout this time, I had been recording audio on my phone. At first, it didn't seem like I captured anything. Going through the recordings the next day, however, I noticed something. Something short but apparent. I isolated the snippet of audio and used an online tool to amplify the volume several times so that it could be heard more clearly. That's when it struck me, it was almost like a growl.

After all this, we hurried back into the house. The three of us left and, again, we saw whatever they were in the yard as we bolted to our cars. Almost a year has passed since those nights and the thought of it all still terrifies me to this day. What's more, as I was out driving the other night, I decided to pass through his neighborhood to sort of reminisce about old times. As I was driving through, I saw those same pale figures, hunched over and moving about. There were about four or five of them. I'm posting this because I'm looking for answers. Any idea as to what we might've seen those nights, please let me know. The events still haunt my memories to this day." NC

The witness states that she encountered a green-eyed crawler humanoid with pale, orange-colored hairless skin. The being became aggressive and attacked the van she was driving. The witness "RJ" contacted me directly in September 2021:

"Hi, Lon. I saw an old post of yours and I am hoping you might have some knowledge to spare.

I need help.

January of this year was a very dark place for me emotionally. My husband and I grew estranged after the loss of our 6-day-old youngest son. For about 2 months, December and January, we were apart as he spiraled with substance abuse to numb the pain. He left town and stayed with his father across the state. When he came back into town, we wanted to see each other.

He checked into a hotel in Bethlehem, Pennsylvania. I drove out to see him around 7 pm when our then two-year-old son fell asleep. We were staying with my mother during this time, and she offered to watch our little one. I stayed for a few hours. It was very emotional, to say the least. We wanted to reconcile and overcome the tragedy we had faced. Around midnight I knew I would have to get back to my mother's house in case our son woke up.

It was pitch black outside, and my GPS led me down a narrow road. I was eager to get home and although very overwhelmed, wide awake due to the adrenaline of seeing my husband for the first time after our 'separation.'

I crossed over a stream and started going slightly uphill. In the middle of the road was a set of bright green eyes. I instantly slowed down because there are a ton of deer in the area. If there is one deer, there is usually more. I slowly crept up the hill in my minivan, scanning for more eyes, and the figure in the middle of the road scuttled to the right-hand side then stayed perfectly still and positioned. Scuttled is the only word to describe the way it moved honestly.

To the right were fields and some trees and brush that lined the perimeter alongside the road. The thing was along with the brush, almost like it was trying to blend in. It was on both its hands and feet. Its arms were unnaturally long and bent at an angle. Its eyes were that reflective green the entire time I drove past it with no pupils. I don't think it looked at me directly, after it positioned itself in the brush it stared past me with a black hole for a mouth, not gaping, but wide open.

Since I slowed down quite a bit to prevent me from hitting what I thought was a deer, I got a good long look at it. It was about 8 feet tall but, on all fours, crouched. Skin looked like orange bark like it was trying to camouflage along with the trees, but it was too orange/tan, and as I crept closer, I saw that it was fleshy. Like gross, orangey swollen bloody fleshy. The nose is what stood out to me most. It was long and pointy; I'd almost compare it to Pinocchio before he would tell a lie. All the same orangey fleshy color. I hope that makes sense. I don't know how else to describe it.

It happened in seconds. I thought I saw a deer, I slowed down as I passed it, and it was NOT a deer. I kept driving. Almost immediately after I laid my eyes on it, I felt my heartbeat in my throat. Such a horrific sense of dread consumed me, and it almost helped me continue to act rationally and drive the hell away from there. I then heard a knocking and a huge thud coming from inside of my van. Like, someone had jumped from the back but on the inside. All my windows were up because it was winter so there was no logical way something could have suddenly appeared as I was driving.

All the hair stood up on the back of my neck, and every instinct I had was telling me to keep staring straight ahead. Do NOT look behind, do NOT look in the rearview mirror, do NOT say a word. So, I didn't. I struggled to breathe. I had a huge lump in my throat as I sped down that road, so beyond scared with every fiber of my being on overdrive telling me to GET AWAY FROM THERE.

The second I turned off that road, that feeling of someone being in the car with me was gone. I looked back and nobody was there. I kept driving and called my husband in hysterics, half-sobbing, half-laughing out of shock, and saying, 'I'm not scared, I'd kick its ass,' because I had a feeling it thrived off of my fear.

It was one of the [most] terrifying things I have ever experienced in my life.

Months have passed since then. My husband and I have since reconciled and have been even stronger since our fallout. We have tried to look more into it, but every time we started to do more research I would get a sick feeling in my stomach, almost like my body was warning me to leave it be. I tried to ignore it and forget it for the longest time.

My husband and I bought a piece of property locally. As we looked at properties, we stayed away from anything big and open with a field because it reminded me too much of that thing. We purchased a heavily wooded lot about 30 miles away from where this experience took place. We are having a home built custom to our 3yo son's needs (our little guy has cerebral palsy). We move onto the property next week in a camper to oversee construction.

But now I'm worried. What if there is another encounter?? And I have my little boy with me this time? What if something bad happens and I lose him? I already lost one son. If anything happened to my oldest, I don't know what I'd do.

We began finally really digging into what that thing was. We investigated the thing itself based on its appearance and the location I saw it at. It turns out that field I saw it at was a part of a memorial park called Housenick Park. There was a lot of Native American history tied into that area, so we dug more into local lore. We came across the term Skinwalker. That was probably the closest thing we found that resembled the creature. That's what we've been referring to it as but there were a few things about my encounter and its appearances that still makes me hesitant to believe with 100% certainty that is what it was." RJ

I talked to RJ by telephone and reassured her that this was, most likely, a onetime encounter.

One of my team, investigator Vincent Richardson, sketched this drawing. RJ verified that the image is very similar to the creature she witnessed.

The description is somewhat different than most humanoid sightings, but I'm convinced it is a crawler humanoid variation.

The local police are called to a residence near Vineland, New Jersey, for a domestic violence complaint. There were a stabbing and other assaults. Not long after, the neighbor witnessed strange "humanoids" around the house. This account was forwarded to me in September 2021:

"So, we've all heard of hauntings and such, but has anyone ever heard of house ghouls? They lurk inside your homes undetected by the naked eye. They live inside the cracks and walls of your home. Mainly crawlspaces, attics, or basements. Not sure if they are supernatural beings or not, but I once encountered them.

The neighbor's house and mine were maybe 80 or 100 feet away when I lived in South Jersey (near Vineland). The neighbors aren't what you would call quiet neighbors. They had the county police out there a couple of times, mainly domestic calls for their adult son from within the home. He may have autism or some other type of learning or developmental disability because he would lash out in anger sometimes in the household. It was just the father and the mother with their son residing there.

One night the ambulance and police came out to the house, and they brought the son out of the home on a stretcher screaming or something. It looked like visible blood, but I really couldn't see anything due to the glare of the police lights and EMS strobes lighting up the area. His mother was also taken to the medical center and his father stayed at the home.

A day or two later, no one was at the home, and it looked like they moved out. It seemed like they just up and left. We're in a little small town also, so I would think somebody would've seen somebody leave. I was able to cure my intense curiosity when a buddy of mine, who I went to high school with, was an EMT that night at the house and I was able to catch him at the local bar.

Sitting at the bar I go up and ask him, 'Oscar, what the hell happened that night?' He calmly looks at me with a grin then responds, 'Crazy.' He told me that the son snapped, took a paring knife, and stabbed his mother in the neck. Then he went after the old man. The father was able to shove his son inside a closet and lock the door until police arrived. While inside the closet the son then started a bellowing scream almost like a howl. When police opened the door, he had taken the paring knife and stabbed all inside his navel then gouged his right eye out. He screamed the whole way out of the home and to the hospital.

I then said, 'Wow, do you think he just snapped?' My friend then said, 'Nah, it's the house.' I then chuckled it off. The same night, later, I saw what looked like people at the home. There was discarded furniture at the end of the lawn for the trash collection. Couches, tables, chairs, and other things I assumed were clothes inside of black trash bags. It's not uncommon for people to search through trash or furniture though. So, as I was going to look away, I noticed these little elderly-like people. They were hunched over, with very skinny bodies and protruding round bellies. Seemed like they were balding with just very thinning strands of cotton-like hair illuminated by the dimming garage light.

I go out to look further and I see two of them rummaging about the trash. One of them then goes around to the side of the house, no more than 4'4" tall stocky build. The skin was like a pale sweaty hide, arms were short at the shoulder and long at the elbows. They also walked with a hobble and disgustingly snorted as it walked. The other was a bit taller, maybe around 5′11″ with short arms, long fingers, and long skinny legs but walked hunched over. If it stood straight up, maybe it would stand around 7 feet. Both had very deep eye sockets. You could barely see any eyes.

In total disbelief of what I'm seeing I had to wake my wife up and show her. She then goes and makes saltwater. She then said an African Orishas prayer, opened the door, poured the water on our doorstep and porch, and closed it. We then watched the things try to get back inside the empty home then they were gone. I later find out that a lady lived there way before I was born, and she charged people to do seances. She was a medium. I don't live around there anymore." D

CANADA

IN SEPTEMBER 2019, I WAS A GUEST ON NOCTURNAL Frequency Radio with Steve Genier and Alex Rondini. During a break, Steve recalled his encounter with a humanoid being one night in Toronto. He later forwarded the information to me, including excerpts from a post that described Steve's encounter.

Steve explains that during the year 2002 he was working a night-shift job that had different shift hours during the week. Steve is also a hiker who takes advantage of every opportunity to be out in the world walking. During his work weeks, he would have nights where his shift ended about 2:00 a.m. Steve would use these work shifts as a chance to walk home late at night when the world was asleep and the night his to enjoy.

During one of these star-bright lovely nights, Steve's shift ended, and Steve started his hour-plus walk home. He listened to his music, enjoyed the beautiful clear quiet night, and started his journey home.

Steve's route took him across a river located near Mississauga in Ontario, Canada. One night Steve set out for his long walk home after finishing his shift that ended at 2 in the morning, which took him straight over the river.

The river had a two-lane bridge over it that Steve walked across on his trek home. The bridge had a grassy knoll down the middle of it that separated the lanes of the bridge.

Steve was starting his way across the bridge when he noticed something ahead of him in the dark. He clearly saw a large animal run from one side of the bridge into the middle of the grassy knoll.

Steve stopped dead in his tracks and instinctively did not move at the sight of something in front of him that he could not identify. Steve stood motionless as he looked at the large silhouette in front of him. At this point, the only thing he could distinguish was that the thing was very large.

Steve stood perfectly still, trying to see what stood about thirty feet in front of him in the dark. As he stood there peering into the night, the thing in front of him began to rise from its four-legged stance until it stood straight up as a human does on two legs.

The thing before him was large, at least 6 feet 5 inches when standing fully erect on two legs. It did not take the stance of a bear or any other animal Steve had ever seen. It looked almost human when standing fully up and still. Steve could make out the semi-human form of this thing as they stood there in the night, peering into the dark at each other.

Steve did not move. The thing did not move either. They stood still for what seemed a very long time to Steve but was only a minute or so. There, alone on the bridge, Steve stood with this thing peering back at him in the night, watching and waiting to see what the other would do next.

Steve could not make out if it had fur or hair or any features on this creature's head. The night would only silhouette the creature by way of the natural light that the stars gave off. It was Canada, near a wooded area over a very dark river in the middle of the night. Only Steve and this thing were to be found out at this time of night. All Steve could see was the dark strange shape of something he had never seen before.

Finally, the thing dropped down to all fours without a sound and took off to continue its way across the grassy knoll to the wooded area across the other side of the bridge.

Steve watched as this large creature continued on its way, running in form somewhat as a dog would run. It ran into the woods back into the night.

Steve stood there motionless for a few moments, waiting and listening to see if the thing left the bridge area. He could not see it or hear any movement and carefully continued his way across the bridge and away from this strange encounter.

Steve felt he was being watched as he made his way as quickly as possible over that bridge and away from the area.

Steve had no idea what he had just seen. He knew there were no bears in the area. The animal was far too large to be a dog or cat type of animal. He did not know of any animal that size that was able to stand erect like a human yet drop to all fours and run like an animal. Steve was also haunted by how this thing looked when it stood up on two legs. Its body was proportioned more like a human form than an animal form. The thing did not have shorter thin-looking legs with a longer body like a deer. The thing did not have the silhouette of a bear. It was far too big and looked nothing like a large dog or cat. Steve knew he had just seen an unknown creature and felt shaken to his core.

Steve has never forgotten this encounter. He has considered over the years, trying to form an investigative team to find out what exactly it is that may be living in the woods in that part of Ontario, Canada.

The Toronto Tunnel Monster has been referenced in sightings and encounters since the late 1970s. Steve's account is as descriptive as any I've read, so I'll stick with his interpretation of this unknown humanoid.

A young camper is approached by a tall pale humanoid while sitting on a trail bench in the Ovens National Park in Nova Scotia at night. Was it a corporeal humanoid? This account was forwarded to me in June 2020:

"Before this incident, I had never had a paranormal experience in my life. That being said, my boyfriend seems to have enough for both of us.

We went camping in the early fall of 2016 at Ovens National Park, Nova Scotia. We had just arrived back from spending the summer in western Canada and hadn't seen each other in four months. So, we decided to spend some time together and go camping with another couple who were close friends of ours. We booked the cheapest cabin at the campground for two nights and headed out.

The first day we spent there was uneventful. To give some context, the park is famous for its sea caves that are carved into the rocky cliffs of the Nova Scotian east shore. The first day we hiked the trail that overlooked the caves (or the Ovens as they were called) and we were able to go down into some of them. That night we had a campfire but turned in early. So, we sat inside the small cabin and started playing cards. My boyfriend was being a sore loser and seemed to be acting kind of strange. He abruptly said he was going for a walk and left the cabin. I was annoyed and just let him go for a while and didn't chase him.

After about half an hour I started to get a bit anxious and called his cell. This is where things started to get weird. He didn't answer at first, but he called me back right away. When I answered he seemed to have calmed down a bit, and I asked him where he was. He said he was sitting on a bench on the trail, then he asked where I was. This confused me a bit because I hadn't left the cabin since he left, and I wasn't likely to since I'm terrified of the dark. I told him this and this suddenly freaked him out. He said he was coming back to the cabin. It was weird because he's generally level-headed and hard to scare.

So after about two to three minutes, I hear running foot-steps coming to the cabin and my boyfriend comes tearing through the door. Then this is what he told me.

He had walked out to the trails to get some fresh air and sat down on one of the benches to look out at the ocean. The moon was bright that night, so everything was illuminated well. Then he said he heard someone walking by and he saw this tall and pale figure stop and look at him, and then continue. For some reason, he assumed this was me coming to look for him, and that's when I called him and told him I was in the cabin. He said, that in retrospect, the figure was inhu-manly tall and pale and couldn't possibly be a person. He was not himself for the rest of the night and didn't seem normal until lunch the next day. Do you have any idea about what this might have been?" LB

This next report was sent to me in June 2020:

"I'll give you some background. My family owns a trailer home that sits on a cliff overlooking Lake Kootenay, in the south of the Canadian province of British Columbia. This trailer was used as a sort of a summer getaway destination, as my parents and I visit for about a week or more each summer. The trailer itself is quite old (it was turned into a home by the previous owners in the 70s), but despite its age, it's still a very enjoyable place to experience the warmest months.

The trailer sits in the middle of a cedar pine forest, with a small clearing on the side facing away from the water to park vehicles, as well as a driveway connecting to the road which is about 110 feet away. The nearest town is roughly a 15-minute drive, and there are no neighbors. I sleep at the opposite end of the trailer (which I call the 'cabin' as there is an additional dining room and porch built onto the trailer), with their bed at the front end and mine at the very back. There are two windows next to where I sleep, with one facing parallel to the lake and the other towards the previously mentioned parking area.

Due to the positioning of our cabin in a mountain valley, around 9 pm in the summer it gets very dark very quickly. Since we sometimes are outside after this time, there's a bright lamp mounted on the front end of the trailer which completely illuminates the porch area (facing the lake) and partially lights the parking area. This creates an orange glow that can get spooky, especially when raining.

Around 11 pm one night, I was still awake sitting in bed and reading. I keep the blinds of the window facing away from the lake open as to provide a little light for reading without having to turn on any inside lamps. The light momentarily gets dimmer, so I glance outside. What I saw was a large, almost glowing white creature that was moving through the semi-lit area, casting a shadow over my window. It had very long and spindly limbs, and I could see contours that looked like emaciated ribs on its side. It was hard to estimate a height because it was moving bent over, in what I can only describe as a crawl. Just looking at it instilled so much fear that I couldn't look away, despite how much I wanted to. The creature moved at a fast-walking pace from the front of the cabin and into the tree line.

At the time, I wanted to believe that it was some form of very sick, hairless bear as we frequently saw bears in the area. Looking back, the limbs were just too long to be a bear and too skinny. Also, I would think a bear with mange would still have some hair or discolored skin, but this creature didn't. It appeared entirely to be a white color, and the light from the lamp reflected off its side making it 'glow' a little.

I wish I could provide any form of evidence that what I saw happened." MO

A couple living in northern British Columbia encounter a tall pale humanoid as they are pulling out of their driveway. There was a later incident as well, so the being is most likely living nearby. This account was forwarded to me in December 2020:

"This happened to me and my boyfriend about two years ago. I decided to offer it because it haunts me to this very day, and I still have nightmares about it.

It was about 2 am one night in September 2018. We live about 25 minutes out of town in northern British Columbia, Canada, and our house is surrounded by the woods. Because it's such a dead road, usually we would pull out of the driveway and then turn on our lights. Why? Just a weird habit I suppose. We both would do it.

So, I'm behind the wheel. I pull out to go left down the road and turn on the high beams. Then we see it.

We see this weird, hairless, pale humanoid creature

crouching in the middle of the road. It almost seemed to be glowing, but that was probably because it was such a pale white and I hadn't turned off my high beams. It whipped its head at us as if it was surprised by our lights turning on. After a second, it shambles across the rest of the road in jerky movements and down into the ditch, which was about 3 feet deep. But that's not it. We both watched as it went down into the ditch, turning around to face us. And it stood up on its back legs, exactly like a human but not quite.

It stood over 5 feet higher than the ditch (taller than our car at the time). And remember the ditch is already 3 feet deep, so this creature was over 7 feet tall. It looked aggressive, hunched at the shoulders, and leaning forward slightly as if to look at the car. And I swear I made eye contact with it. No. It was not watching us drive by. It wasn't looking at the car. It was looking through the window, and it was looking right at me! Whatever it was, it was intelligent and knew that the car wasn't moving. It knew we were inside.

I drove so slowly, turning my head and keeping eye contact with it as we drove past and it did the same, craning its neck to watch me leave. My boyfriend couldn't see it past me at that point. Eventually, it's out of my vision and I look back at the road.

We are both completely silent. I'm driving less than 10km an hour, having taken my foot off the gas when I saw something in the road. To this day I don't really tell people because they just laugh it off or try to explain it as an albino starving bear or something.

Now, this year (2020) his parents were visiting just before winter hit. They have a dog. I and his mom were having a smoke on the deck, which is about 6 feet off the ground. It's dusk. Not much light. We were on the left side of the deck, the same side we turn on the road to go to town. You can see the patch of woods where the creature would have been before, so this instance happened in the same little area.

I hear a bunch of cracking twigs just as the dog goes nuts. The dog is small, so we were surprised when he almost jumped off the deck to run in the woods. My boyfriend comes out just in time and we see, just beyond some trees so it's obscured, a tall, lanky white form. But we couldn't see anything else definitive, and his mom has terrible eyesight and didn't have glasses. I KNOW it was the same creature. I got this twisting feeling in my gut.

We don't leave our house at night. Maybe it's weird but I want to see it again. I used to think, 'Wow, these stories are cool. I so believe in them.' It was nothing compared to the awed terror I felt when I made eye contact with something I'm positive is not natural.

I think about it every single day and it can bring me to tears because it scares me so much." C

A British Columbia resident has had several encounters with a white humanoid with light-colored hair. It abruptly appears, then vanishes. Is it a corporeal being or something different? This account was sent to me in June 2021:

"I've been having encounters with a humanoid 'thing' in the woods behind my place. The woods behind my house are quite extensive so it's not just a strip of trees. The first encounter I had was when I had shot a raccoon that had been getting in the garbage and spreading it all over the yard. I took it back into the woods to dump the carcass and I arrived at a clearing that's a short walk from my house. Once I knelt to get a better grip on it to toss it into a large ditch, I caught something in the corner of my eye. I turned to see what it was and just standing there was what appeared to be some weird person in the tree line facing my direction with a candle at about upper abdomen level. I am not the best at estimating the height of something from a distance, but it was taller than me by a good bit (I am 6'1"). The only reason why I could see it is because of the light source it was holding. I looked down for a second to see what I was doing and when I looked back up it was gone. I had only looked away for a fraction of a second.

At this point, I had decided to get out of there and just left after dropping everything. Ever since then I have been seeing this thing standing completely still in random locations around the woods and when I look away 'poof,' it's gone.

Well, tonight, I took my dog out back and immediately felt like something was off and got my flashlight and looked around, not going in any further than my pup. There it was, standing completely still, so still that it looked like the wind wasn't even disturbing what appears to be its hair. After staring at this thing not moving or making any noise, it lifted an appendage in the direction of the dog. My pup eventually vanished into the darkness which is the point where it lifted what appeared to be an arm in his last known direction of travel. After a staring contest with whatever it is, it lowered its arm, and my dog came back running out of the woods back to the door. I wasn't going to lose sight of this thing while I was so close, so I backed up still facing it with my light on it. I got back to the door and turned around for a second to get inside, and when I turned around to shut the door, it was much closer. I shut the door and closed all the blinds as soon as I could.

It has never done anything like this before and has never been anywhere near my house let alone in my backyard before. At this point, I'm worried about what could happen especially now that it appears to be getting more aggressive and is stalking me.

It's very tall and appears to have some sort of material on it that's white in color. It's always looking straight down. Lighter-colored hair. The hair is longer and from what I've seen only on its head.

The most significant incident was the first time and the last time which happened to be last night before I wrote this post. These incidents were a year and a half apart with random other incidents scattered in between. Every time I've seen it has been deeper in the woods, never this close to the house.

As for witnesses, the only other person who's seen it is my friend on one occasion and it was when we were both in the woods together. It seemed to be at a greater distance than usual in this incident.

I haven't recorded it because it hasn't ever been in the same place, and as soon as I take my eyes off it, 'poof,' it's gone. As for the reason for not going inside to grab my phone last night, I'm not just going to leave my dog out there with whatever it is so I can go viral on the internet for a 'spooky ghost encounter.' I am setting up deer cams today to see if it ends up in my yard again as I will not be going out there again to find out." CG

This "humanoid" post is quite interesting and somewhat different than the standard fare. From what I have gathered, this individual lives in British Columbia, but not sure of the specific area. The real question is if this is a corporeal being or a manifestation. Hard to tell, even though it appears to have supernatural abilities. Very strange account.

This next account was forwarded to me in November 2018.

It's a third-person description of an incident on an Ontario, Canada, farm by the witness' American friend:

"This incident occurred in May 2015 in Dufferin County in Ontario, Canada. A friend of mine recently recounted this strange story to me. This friend owns a few hundred acres of land which he rents to farmers to grow crops. As you can imagine the area is rather quiet, not too many houses or traffic around these back roads. His house was under renovation at the time, so he was staying in a trailer around the back of his property. Nothing but potato field with an old barn poking out from the fields.

One night, he said around 1 am, he was woken up to his dogs going nuts, scratching at the trailer door. When he went to let them out, he was surprised to see bright yellow lights behind and inside the nearby barn. Thinking it was trespassers, he let his dogs loose and went to grab his rifle. He said as he was loading it, he heard his dogs go from barking to yelping and whining. They came barreling back into the trailer and proceeded to hide under the table.

Thinking these people hurt his dogs, he stepped out of the trailer and fired five rounds into the air and began yelling as he readied another magazine. He got a response when the lights around the barn grew incredibly bright. He admits that at that point he was pretty freaked out. He said that he stood there for a bit staring at the lights when he noticed two beings casually walking across the field towards the barn.

Apparently, when he saw them, he was hit with a mixture of confusion and fear. He describes them as humanoid, pale white, tall, and thin. Having very small heads in comparison to their bodies, he also notes that they must have been 6'5" with most of that height being leg length. He stated that they moved very strangely. Their upper body seemed stiff and locked, but their legs moved very fluidly. Almost bringing their knees to their chest. Understandably fear took over him, he took aim and fired three rounds at the beings. Which just made them completely stop moving. Then he noticed the third one to his left very close but walking away from his trailer. He turned around, went back inside, and went for his handguns when the light outside vanished. He sat inside his trailer with silent dogs until morning.

He didn't check out the barn until two days later. He found nothing strange there. No burn marks, no holes, all was normal. When checking the fields, he also found absolutely nothing. He told me that he was freaked out for a while afterward, but nothing strange has ever happened on his property since then.

He also likes to add that not too far from his property is a large piece of military land in the woods. It's completely fenced off with barbed wire and sports nothing but vents sticking out of the ground inside it. Apparently, it's a site used for listening to and broadcasting messages into space.

So that's the story, I was curious to find out what other people think this might have been. And I know, I didn't tell it too well. If there are any questions, I'll be sure to ask him and get back to you." SD

SD proceeded to answer questions and provide follow-up information:

"I did ask him quite a bit. Unfortunately, he only saw the two from the side at a distance, and the third was walking with its back turned to him.

He said that he couldn't see anything on the two far ones' faces. But the one with the back turned to him appeared to have no ears. He also notes that they had small rounded almost cone-shaped heads. Apparently small enough to look odd on their already thin bodies.

As for human characteristics, from what he could tell, they did not look unhealthy. They were extremely thin and tall, but they did not look unnatural. 'From what I could tell, they didn't look starving. It looked right for them.'

On top of that, he states that they appeared to have no hands or feet. Their limbs seemed to end in stubs.

But that's all I could really get out of him about their appearance. Understandably, he didn't study them all that well." SD

This account caught my eye because of a report I received several years earlier describing similar beings observed in Grand Valley, Ontario, which is also in Dufferin County. I don't know if it's related, but it's an interesting side note.

The following account was sent to me in April 2020:

"These incidents occurred during my teenage years, at 16 years old. I lived in a small town of 2000 people, mainly surrounded by boreal forest, in a region of Québec, Canada. This place was great, as we often saw deer and it was usually a quiet and safe place. To put this in a bit of context, my house was located at the side of a dead-end and the only light source at night was from the house. There was a single street-light at the end of the road, but it only lit a part of the street and the forest behind it.

We were a dog family. I only had small dogs when I lived there. Every day we needed to let them out, as all dogs do. But at night they were almost impossible to see because of the darkness. Our terrain was kind of big and the light sources were weak.

I was a gamer at that time, and I was often up late. So, I

was the one who needed to take out the dog at 2 am because it stayed with me while I was playing. One night I opened the door and waited for my dog to do his thing while trying to look at it. I only was able to see the reflection on the light in its eyes when it looked at me. I started to look around because there were sometimes deer roaming in the woods under the streetlight or wild turkeys moving around when a little dark spot caught my attention. It looked like a human head coming out of the bushes, but I couldn't see it because it was a bit in the dark. I didn't want my dog to run after whatever it was (it tended to run away after wild animals), so I called it. It didn't listen to me but the thing in the bushes started to crawl towards the street slowly. It looked like a human, with thin limbs but a normal body and a slightly longer neck.

I started to freak out a bit and shook the treats cup so my dog would hurry. It came inside running and I shut the door as fast as I could. I turned off the lights in my house so I could have a view of what was outside. The strange being crawled fast, almost running like a dog with every limb broken, as an improvised crawling movement. The being passed under the light, where I saw it had no fur, like a shaved animal. It was disgusting. I was afraid and standing in the dark. The being ran towards the light and continued [to] the street, where I couldn't see it because the houses in my neighborhood were delimited by trees. I locked the door and went to sleep with my dog. I talked to nobody about it.

A couple of months later I went to bed kind of early one night (11:00 pm) and went to watch some videos on my phone. These were gaming videos and I had earphones on. A sound on the video was recurring and I thought it was annoying, like a distant weird scream.

After a couple of minutes, the video finished and I went to see another, but during the loading, the sound occurred again. I took off my earphones and waited for the sound. I heard it and immediately had tears in my eyes. It was coming from my window. My room was on the second floor, so I looked down in the forest if there was some movement. The only light near the forest entrance was the moonlight and an underwater light in our pool that emitted a small halo around it. I couldn't see anything, but the sound occurred again. It was like a mix between a distorted scream and a pig having his throat slit, or a strong pain whining from a dog. I looked down and saw something that passed so fast it was hard to see it, but I barely saw a human-sized being with thin limbs crawling like a spider. It wasn't running after anything, but the sound occurred another time. It was the most horrible thing I ever heard. I closed my window quickly. I heard it again three other times, and it stopped after that.

I talked to my dad about the sound, and he told me it was probably a deer being attacked by a wild animal. I was so scared of it I barely walked in the woods at night the following 3 years, before moving to a city to go to a university.

Even to this day I have never heard of an animal or being like that. There were barely any reports of wolves, coyotes, or bears in my area, and believe me, I made a lot of discoveries exploring the forest in this town." AB

REPORTS FROM AROUND THE WORLD

FROM THIS POINT FORWARD, I WILL PRESENT A PLETHORA of accounts that may be classified by some investigators, readers, and enthusiasts as "non-terrestrial" or simply "otherworldly." The reason why I am including them is to offer you a variety of unexplained humanoid encounters and sightings that witnesses are reporting.

I will also include a few last-minute accounts that I received just before the book was presented for publishing.

Possibly the first written account referencing an alien, or a possible humanoid encounter is a story in Japanese folklore. The story takes place on February 22 in the spring of 1803. Offshore from a beach called Hara-yadori in the territory of Ogasawara Etchuu-no-kami (4000 koku), who occupied a position named "Yoriai-seki" of Tokagawa shogunate at that time, a kind of boat was observed from the beach. People approached this boat using their small boats and eventually caught it. They towed it to the beach.

The boat was round and resembled a kind of kou-hako (a box used to burn incense). Its diameter was more than 3 ken (5.45 meters). On the upper part of the boat, there were glass-fitted shoji (windows with lattice), and they were shielded by chan (a kind of waterproofed putty made from pine-tree gum). The bottom of this ship was reinforced by separated iron plates. This structure may protect the boat from destruction by sunken rocks. Since the glass-fitted shoji were transparent, the people could see the inside of the boat, where they found a woman with strange features. Her hair and eyebrows were red, and her face was pink. It seemed that long white hair was added to her original hair.

This foreign woman held one square box whose size was about two shaku (60 cm) in her hands. It seemed that this box was very important to her because she held this box constantly, and she prohibited anyone from approaching it.

The objects found in this boat were investigated by the people. There was about two shou (3.6 liters) of water in the small bottle. There were two pieces of carpet, cake-like food, and kneaded meat. While people discussed what to do about this boat, the woman observed them peacefully.

Another similar description of, possibly, the same incident was found for March 24, 1803. A strange boat drifted ashore on a beach named Haratono-hama in Hitachi state in Japan. The boat was hollow, and its shape was like a rice-cooking pot. It had a kind of rimmed edge at the center-level part of the boat. In the part above this edge, the boat was painted in black and had four small windows on four sides. All shoji (windows with lattice) were shielded by chan (a kind of waterproof putty made from pine-tree gum). The lower part of the boat was reinforced by steel bars. These bars looked to be made of Western-made iron of the highest quality. The height of the boat was one jyou, two shaku (3.64 m), and its diameter was one jyou, eight shaku (5.45 m).

A woman (or girl) was found inside this boat, and her age appeared around twenty. She was about five shaku (1.5 m) tall, and her skin was white as snow. Her long hair vividly hung on her back. Her facial features were incomparably beautiful. Her clothes were strange and unrecognizable, and her language was not understood by anyone. She held a small box in her hands and prohibited anyone from approaching this box.

One of the earliest press reports that I received of these pale humanoids originated in Mexico. The information was released very soon after the events.

In April 2010, residents of Colonia Chinameca, Mexico, were gripped with fear after two children reported seeing an alleged monster of humanoid characteristics and four legs on Calle Londres in that busy sector.

The children described the entity as a little man with smooth, gray skin and four legs or lower extremities. It was seen in an empty lot of the street in question in the Chinameca district.

Both children (thirteen years old each) and residents were terrified and spread the word of the "being" they had just seen among other locals. The mother of one of the youngsters, seeing the state of nerves that her child was in, called the police, requesting that whoever caused her son to fall into such a state of terror be apprehended.

After receiving the report, law enforcement agents reported to the scene and searched everywhere for the strange little man but could not establish its whereabouts. However, this is not the first time that strange things have been reported in this district, according to the residents.

It was later learned that a gray-colored, four-legged humanoid submerged into the waters of the Monclova River at the location known as "El Charco Azul." Public Safety Personnel reported immediately to the scene to deal with the case, which represents the second sighting of an unknown being with matching characteristics. Officers of the Policia Preventiva ordered bathers out of the water at the location where the "grey monster" was seen entering the river.

According to reports provided by the police department, residents contacted the desk officer to report the strange humanoid sighting at 2:00 p.m.

The next day, four young men from Colonia del Río were terror-stricken by the "little man" while fishing for king prawns at the location.

The monster appears to dwell in the city's southwestern section, over by Ejido Curva de Juan Sánchez, where it was reported to have slain ten goats over the past six months and has been seen on at least five occasions, even in broad daylight.

A twenty-one-year-old shepherd from Irapuato, Guanajuato, says that he has seen the strange beast several times between Ejido Curva de Juan Sánchez and the Colinas de Santiago district. The beast is no ordinary animal and is also capable of extremely high leaps.

The Mexican press does tend to report unusual incidents in a tabloid style. But I found, through subsequent research, that the information on these sightings was substantiated.

Two friends were vacationing in Cuba along the Playa Ancon coast. One night they encountered an unknown glowing white figure on the beach near their hotel. I received this report in August 2020:

"Last year a friend and I went to Cuba for vacation. We were on the Playa Ancon coast. It was New Year's Day, around 3 am when it happened.

After a night of drinking and dancing, we decided to go to the beach for a little bit. It was nearly pitch-black outside, and we were just walking around on the shore talking and looking at the stars. Suddenly my friend calls my name and tells me to look down the shore. What we saw was a radiantly glowing white figure, about 300 meters away. It had long legs and a head, standing about 7 feet. I immediately thought of the Fresno Nightcrawler, though at the time I didn't know what it was called (we nicknamed it the Ocean Alien).

My friend said that before I had seen it, it was just standing there, and for a moment it looked as though it had stepped into the water, submerged completely, and then stepped back onto the beach. We stared at it for a couple of moments, and then it started taking slow steps towards us. We both got so scared, and we booked it back to our hotel room without looking back. We were both rattled so we didn't sleep for most of the night.

The next few days of our trip we asked guests and employees at our hotel about what we saw. We even went to the city closest to our hotel and asked a bunch of locals, and nobody knew what we were talking about or could provide any possible explanations for what we saw. We even went back to the beach a few other nights around the same time but never saw it again.

Unfortunately, we were both so frightened by the 'Ocean Alien,' neither of us thought to take our phones out and take any photos or video. Does anybody have any idea of what it could have been? I've done some research about Cuban folklore and cryptid sightings and haven't found anything even remotely similar." AS

In March 2013, I received an email that included three screenshots from a trail camera of an unknown bright white humanoid. Here is the text from the email:

"Hey, Lon. I run a paranormal investigation group out of mid-Michigan. Recently, we had a member, who received from a friend, these eerie photos off a trail cam. According to his story, this photo was taken in Alpena, Michigan, which is in the upper part of the mitten. Any thoughts on what this may be?" TV

Below are the three screenshots that I received. After substantial analysis, the figure does not appear to have been digitally altered. To this day, there has been no clear-cut evidence as to what this humanoid was.

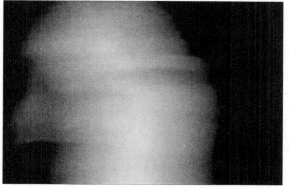

I received the following account from a young woman in Scotland in September 2018:

"Me and my friend were walking around a massive park in my town in Scotland and it was around 11 pm. We were just walking around having a smoke and a laugh, being young and stuff. By this point it was pitch black. There are no lights in the park and I'm a bit on edge because I'm not keen on the dark and I was kind of paranoid from the weed, but I'm going to just cut to the interesting part.

So, me and my friend, let's call him Sam, walk towards the actual swing park within the park and we're like 10 metres from the park. There's this unexplainable rancid smell that physically caused me to gag. We joke and say something about it being this girl from school we don't like and head into the park. The smell is only getting stronger, and I glance over at the small wall surrounding the park. There's a bench and squatting behind the bench, at least 1.5 metres tall squatting, was what looked like a freakishly tall guy. He appeared to be naked and hairless. We both kind of stared for a minute before looking at each other as if to say 'Yo, you can see that right' and the thing started laughing like a 4-year-old girl. We got the hell out of there and ran like our lives depended on it and went home. We just laughed it off and kind of forgot about it, at least Sam forgot about it. But it was weeks ago, and I'm still spooked and refuse to go near that park after dark.

The park is massive and heavily wooded too. What's weird is that I've smoked there for years and never ever saw something like that or heard anyone mention them here. It would have been at least 2.5 metres tall. It was very pale white gray in colour and I think that it was that thing that was giving off the smell. I haven't heard any local folklore or urban legends about anything like this. I don't know if it just wandered and ended up here or if they're migrating here or something. Overall was scary and will haunt me forever! Can you help me figure out what I saw?" LL

This next account, with a sketch, was received in February 2019:

"This happened when I lived in a children's home in a more remote part of the town in Finland. It was at the start of winter, around the end of December 2017. The house is in the woods but has many houses close to each other. I had to walk to a side road in the woods to smoke my cigarette since it wasn't allowed to smoke on the property. It was already dark, but the road was dimly lit by the lights of one of the houses. This is the part I always felt uneasy walking. I was almost back at the house when I started feeling uneasy again, but this time it was intense. I felt something watching me.

I heard a branch break and some leaves crunching and saw this bizarre-looking thing walking from the woods over the road and back to the woods on the other side of the road. It was pale grey, on all fours, but the legs were weird, like humanoid but at the same time the knees were bent like a dog. The front legs were mostly the same but not so bent. The body was slim, and the back was kind of arched, like upwards. The head and face are so hard to describe. It was kind of humanoid too but had no human features or ears. I focused mainly on the legs because they looked so wrong. It didn't make any sounds or didn't smell like anything. I was close enough to see details but not close enough to smell.

I stood there, as my heart was pounding, and I wanted to scream and run home, but I couldn't because the thing was on the way. It was slow too, like the average human speed when walking.

After it was gone, I ran back home and told a friend who

told me he always felt uneasy there. What could it be? I want some answers. I tried to draw it." DK

An eyewitness recounts a strange encounter with a tall white being in a British Columbia forest. Is it a legendary creature known by the First Nations people or something else? This account was received in March 2020:

"My friend and I had an encounter with a tall white being in his backyard and it still scares me to this day. It was swaying silently back and forth, and I felt like I was going to die. I showed someone who is First Nations my experience and my drawing and they told me the name of what they call them. I did some research, and it turns out several different First Nations cultures have names for these beings. I strongly believe these people witnessed the same thing especially because it took place during a 'drumming ceremony.' This is the first time I have read anything that has come close to what I and my friend saw, and I strongly believe they saw the same being or a variation of it.

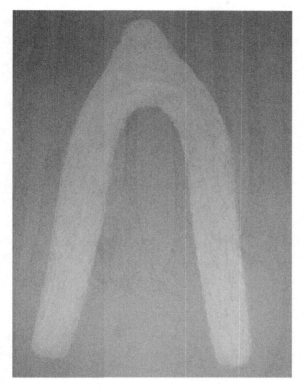

The witness provided this sketch.

Here is what happened. I entered my friend's backyard 5-acre forest at night. It was close to 1 am and both of us imme-diately saw something out of place down the path below about 30–40 feet away from us in between the trees. It was tall and appeared to be completely white and soft like light, but it did not illuminate the trees or ground around it. There was no face or any facial features we could see, no arms and it was shaped in an upside-down V or U. It was 7–8 feet in height, and making creepy swaying movements with its whole body, two legs left to right, back and forth silently while standing on the forest floor in the same spot the whole time we saw it. It was so white that you could see the shadow being cast while it was swaying. It did not pick up its legs or walk at all. It was beautiful to look at but terrifying at the same time.

We watched it in silence as it was swaying, and I started to feel impending doom (the sinking feeling in your chest) set in and it felt like I was going to die or something bad was going to happen. I told my friend specifically 'I don't like this.' He agreed, and we immediately left the forest. We went back in the morning and there was nothing out of the ordinary in the spot where we saw this being." PT

A Queensland, Australia, woman relates her many sightings and encounters since she was a child, with what she believes to be a crawler humanoid. Was it following her? This account was received in May 2021:

"I don't sleep with curtains open because of crawler humanoids. I'm a grown woman and I still can't sleep at night with the curtains open. In fact, when I moved into my current house, I installed dual curtain rods so that even if my light-blocking curtains are open, there's a layer of privacy sheers behind them to block any sight.

I have seen the crawler four times. I now live in Brisbane, Queensland. I don't truly know if it's the same one, they were all seen at different locations. It's been years since I last saw one, but I still feel like they were the same creature, or at least, they knew me.

The first time, I was a very small child. Perhaps 4, maybe

5. My house was an old-style flood house, so it was technically two stories tall but under the house was where we kept the car and our laundry room. Upstairs was where the living areas were. We were one of the only houses there, it was in the early days of the town and there were only a few other houses on the cul de sac. The back of our property was maybe 500 meters from the ocean, but you couldn't see or hear the coastline from the house. There were some light rainforests surrounding our fully fenced house. My bedroom faced the back of the property.

I woke up one night, which wasn't unusual for me because I was a very light sleeper. This night, my parents hadn't closed my curtains. When I looked towards my window, I could see it. Keep in mind, I was on the second floor.

It was looking through my window. I couldn't see much, the only light was coming from outside, but I could see the silhouette of its body. It was pale and thin but still, the frame of the creature was huge, easily 2 meters tall. It was hanging off my roof, holding on to the frame of my window, and even though I couldn't see its face I just KNEW it was looking at me. I was terrified. It's been almost two decades since I saw it, but I can still remember the intense fear I felt. It took me so much courage to get out of bed and walk to my parents' room, where I finally fell back asleep. My parents told me it was just a dream.

The next time I remember seeing it, I was probably about 7 or so. I had moved houses probably a few months before, and my new house (about a 16-hour drive from my old place, still in Queensland) was a single-story home, but still on the coast of the country. It was a lot further from the ocean, about 5 km, but very much the same kind of area. We were one of the only houses in the area and I had no neighbours.

I woke up one night because I heard something banging against the metal fence. In Australia, we have a brand that makes fences and roofs out of corrugated metal that's been painted. They're quite common, 6 feet high cream-coloured metal fences. And they make an unmistakable noise when something hits them. I have no idea how anything could climb one of these fences. They're completely smooth with nothing to grab onto. Even in my teens, I tried sneaking out by jumping the fence and I just slid right down again.

At first, when I woke up, I thought some birds must have landed on the fence, but the noise continued for longer than it would take a bird to land. My next thought was that someone was trying to break into the house. I turned over in bed to face the window and saw it. Well, I didn't see it at first. It was very dark out and I don't remember much of a moon. As my eyes adjusted, I could only just make out the figure hunched down in front of my window. Even in the hunched-down pose, it was still huge. This time I didn't run to my parents. Their bedroom was no longer across the hall, it was all the way on the opposite side of the house, and I'd have to pass so many uncovered windows to get there. I don't remember when I fell asleep, but I eventually woke up in the morning, and once again my parents told me I must have been dreaming. However, from then on, they always came into my bedroom and closed my blinds before bed.

The next time I saw it, I was 9. I know I was 9 because I had just moved schools and made friends with a girl who we'll call Casey. She invited me to stay at her house one night, and I was so excited. She was the first friend I'd made since moving schools and it had been ages since I'd gotten to have a sleepover. Everything went great, the night was perfectly normal, and I woke up in the middle of the night to the sound of Casey crying. I sat up in bed and asked her what was wrong. She pointed towards the window, where I saw the thing again. Unfortunately for me, Casey had a night light, and I could see much more of the creature than I ever had before. It looked so crusty and dry. It was almost totally white, devoid of any real identifying features, except it stared at us with black eyes and mouth agape. Casey's window was small, and it had to hunch down to see us.

We both got up and ran crying to her mum. She turned on the outside light and brought us back inside the bedroom and pointed out a large gumtree outside the window that she tried to explain must have been what we saw. We argued with her, the thing we saw was right against the window, not several meters away, and it wasn't to the left, it was to the right. Casey's mom eventually let us sleep on the couch.

A couple of months later, Casey stayed over at my house. When I woke up in the morning Casey was gone. I asked my parents, and they told me that Casey had gotten up in the night and started crying, begging to go home. When I saw her again on Monday at school, she told me she got up at night to go to the bathroom, and when she walked past the lounge room, she could see the 'tall skin monster' crawling through the trees at the bottom of my backyard. She never came to my house again, and I lost touch when I moved schools a year later.

I don't know what it was I saw. It can't have been sleep paralysis, I was able to move and speak and everything. And it wasn't a dream because someone else saw it.

I don't know if this relates in any way, but when my partner moved into my house a few months ago, he opened the curtains one night before bed. This time it was a full moon. I had already fallen asleep. I'm now living in a two-story house with my bedroom on the second floor again.

I woke up in the middle of the night to my partner getting

up and closing the curtains. When I asked him why, he told me he had a nightmare that there was a tall, skinny, white man clinging onto my roof, almost like a spider, and it was peering into my bedroom. He said it must have been a hallucination (he had been up all night playing video games) and when he got up from bed it jumped back onto the roof. I still haven't told him, but his description of what he saw is exactly what I saw the first time I saw the crawler. Only, now I'm living in a busy neighbourhood with plenty of houses, unlike past experiences where I've been one of the only houses on the block and surrounded by forests.

I have heard 'mimicking' many times but have always drawn it up to the imagination. Sometimes I will hear my partner walk into the room and say hello at night but when I roll over, I see the light coming down the hallway and I realise that he's still in the lounge room on the computer. I've heard my mother's voice a few times too. Throughout my childhood in all the homes I've lived in, we've had issues with dogs barking at nothing, and security motion detector lights randomly coming on at night when nobody is there. I don't know if those two things are related or not but I've heard similar happenings in crawler-related stories before and thought I'd mention it.

So those are my stories. I don't know if I've seen a crawler, or something else, or if I've seen anything at all." PM

A South Carolina man was taking an evening walk in the woods near his home when he encounters a pale crawler humanoid. The entity continuously stalked and cackled at the witness. The account was forwarded to me in August 2021:

"I'll start by saying I've never believed in anything paranormal. I'm a pretty science-based dude. I always look for a logical explanation, and I still am for this encounter. So, if you have any ideas let me know.

I live just south of Charleston, South Carolina. I don't have much time for leisure with work the past year. I've been having to accept some awful shifts to get by with COVID times. So, I've lost my ability to go on my evening walks which are a method of stress relief for me. It had been a while since I had gone on one, so 3 nights ago I decided to just go for a late-night walk. I put on my headband flashlight and decided to take a path I hadn't in ages. There's a small trail near the back of my neighborhood that goes about 4 miles deep into the woods. I planned to walk about 1.5 miles in and take the parallel path to come back.

I make it down to around 1.3 miles (according to my Fitbit) and I start getting that feeling I'm being watched. I turn off my head light and sit still to listen. At this point I'm more concerned there's a guy following me who is up to no good. I heard clear footsteps in the leaves off the trail and they've been behind me for nearly 5 minutes. I stopped, thinking it was an animal or another walker, and became worried. Sitting there for probably 3–4 minutes and I hear nothing at all. I turn back on my head light and decide to start walking quickly back home.

About two minutes later I hear footsteps again. This time it sounds different. Sounds like 4 feet instead of 2 feet walking. And it's walking at the same increased speed I am. I turn around quickly with my head light and my phone light and point it behind me. Silence. I get angry and yell out, 'Leave me alone. I'm going to call the cops, and if you come at me, I have a knife!' Silence. I yell again and then roll out of here and start walking towards where I heard the walking. About 20 yards out (hard to fully make out because the flashlight doesn't reach too far) I see what looks like a literal naked man running full speed on all fours into the woods. And some details lead me to believe it wasn't a person.

For one, it was damn near hairless. Completely bald, pale white skin, and the way it ran on [all] 4s looked natural. Not like when you try to run on all 4s and look stupid. It looked like its bone structure was designed to walk on all 4s. There was no hunched look, the back was flat, and it was FAST. Last thing that happened was straight out of a horror movie.

I hadn't heard anything in a while on my way back but kept turning around to be sure. With about .5 miles left to go until I was in the clear I hear a MAD dash through the leaves. I whip around and it stops on a dime. I see the edges of its head behind a tree. I yell loudly to try to intimidate [it]. What I heard next I'll never forget in my entire life. It cackled like a monkey. A noise I've only heard in nature documentaries. The tone was that of mockery, a predator having fun with me. I didn't stick around. I sprinted as fast as possible back home.

I'd love to believe this was some prank, or some rabid, bald, diseased coyote. But I got a clear look at it. It wasn't. It had human feet and human hands. A human head and a human buttock. But nothing else about it was human. I called the cops after and told them a man was following me. I didn't want to say some creature because they'd think I'm crazy. They didn't find anything, but they did see quite a bit of activity in the leaves and dirt about 50 feet from where the trail was, leading far back into the woods before it got to a large stretch of grass, where no footprints were seen.

Please someone tell me I'm crazy or that this was some elaborate prank or deformed man." TA

A central Indiana couple is riding around late one night in June 2020 when they encounter a pale crawler humanoid crossing the road in front of them. I received this report in August 2021:

"Earlier in 2020, when the lockdown was going on, my girlfriend and I were getting bored sitting around. So sometimes during the day or later at night, we would just hop in my car and drive around and chat.

Well, one night, around 12:45–1 am, we were driving this back road by her house that's just trees and forest for miles. The road was empty, and there are no houses, so I have my high beams on going around a corner. As soon as the road straightened out, I slammed [on] my brakes and saw an almost pure white creature in the middle of the road. I only caught a glimpse, but it was squatting with long legs, super long arms, and an incredibly humanoid figure. The posture it had while squatting was very human-like, except its elbows almost touched the pavement.

My girlfriend screamed and within a second of seeing it, it ran on all fours like a blur to a tree by the road, and just jumped into it. The area of the tree it landed in was at least 15–20 feet off the ground, and when it jumped, I could see it slightly stretch out.

I've driven by that area a lot since then and haven't seen it again since. Anyone else seen something similar? I didn't see any teeth, the head was human-shaped, and its face was long. Blackish sunk in eyes, long nose and its mouth was closed. It ran away and hid in that tree as if it knew it shouldn't be seen, but it didn't seem animalistic. I'd say at least 6.5–7 feet in length. It looked directly at the car before it ran, and it was incredibly thin, almost boney, and yes, its thighs and calves were long.

This occurred in June of 2020. I honestly don't know the

road. It's near US-37 and 191st St. in Noblesville, Indiana, in Hamilton County at around 12:45–1 am." TG

A third party relays an account told to them by the experiencer, involving an encounter and attack by a crawler humanoid. This was an intense incident. This report was forwarded to me in August 2021:

"The setting is an extremely rural house in eastern Kentucky, the kind of place where you would have to drive 20 miles to get to civilization. A young girl around the age of 10 is playing fetch with a 90-pound German Shepherd police dog that had just been retired from the force. The girl threw the ball, and it hit a tree to her right, sending it behind her. The dog charged off behind her to get the ball. Just then, the dog's body was thrown past her and hit a tree with a loud thud, knocking it unconscious. Then a hard object slammed into the back of her head, knocking her out. When she awoke, she recognized the terrain and knew she was in the deep woods. She also felt her body getting dragged along the forest floor, pulled by the back of her hair.

The young girl screamed, scaring whatever was dragging her, making the entity drop her. She then ran off back in the direction of her home. She turned her head to see a white, pale, emaciated figure with black eyes chasing [her] after rapidly gaining ground. The crawler caught up to the little girl and grabbed the front of her hair with her kicking and screaming into the woods. The little girl struggled in vain to get away, but the animal was too strong for her.

The crawler dragged her into a riverbed and dunked her head in the water, attempting to drown her. Then she heard a loud cracking sound loud enough to be heard under the water, and the crawler let go of her. She pulled her head out of the water to see her police dog with its vise-like jaws firmly clamped around the crawler's upper forearm. The arm hung limp, and she could tell it had been broken. The crawler tried and failed to lift the dog but lacked the strength to do so. She then ran off back home, leaving her dog to fight the crawler. Her parents consulted her and believed her story. A day later and the dog hadn't returned. Another day passed, and still no dog. Then on the evening of the third day, her dog hobbled out of the woods, its body covered in cuts and lacerations. It also had a lot of caked blood around its mouth. That dog made a full recovery and ended up living three years after its fight with the crawler.

This story confirms the idea that these animals are fragile in comparison to other cryptids. And if the dog was able to take down the crawler, which wouldn't surprise me as a 90-pound German Shepherd can take down a 300-pound man. Then perhaps they are even weaker than we thought." SW

A pale grey humanoid is observed on the side of a road, crouched down beside a telephone pole. When the high beams illuminated the being, it quickly scampered unnaturally up the pole. I received this account in August 2021:

"Last year, on Saturday, June 27th, my paranoia was at its peak. My friends wanted me to come to pick them up, go to McDonald's in the nearest town, and then drive around on country roads. Because of my paranoia, I had my mom walk me outside to my car, and I had my dad watch out through the window to make sure my mom was safe going back into the house. I also had them lock the doors. My paranoia was bad that entire summer.

I picked up my friends, went to McDonald's, and started riding around country roads. This is something we did often because there's not much to do in our village in the St. Louis Metro East.

We were coming back into town sometime between just after midnight, and we noticed the moon appeared red. We started talking about it, and we began arguing about what effects a red moon has on people. Just as we started getting loud, we saw a creature on the side of the road. It seemed to be humanoid, but its forearms were much longer than its upper arms. It was very pale, almost greyish with no hair. The fingers were very long and pointy, maybe claws? It also appeared to be very malnourished, we could see its ribcage. It was crouched down next to a telephone pole, just as we were coming into town. I slammed on the brakes and turned on my high beams to get a better look at the being. It looked at us, and then zoomed up the pole faster than what should be physically possible. It was like a beam of light. We all went silent and started discussing what we had just seen. We all agreed that we had seen the same thing. All our descriptions were the same.

Just up the road was the friend's house we were going to. They had to run in to grab some stuff, so I stayed in the car with the doors locked and my eyes closed. When they came back outside, we backed out of the driveway to head to my house (which is right down the street) and we saw it behind us, standing in the middle of the road, looking at us. My house is only a couple of blocks away, so when we got there, we ran inside as fast as we could. We locked the doors and stayed at my house for a while before I eventually gave them a ride back to his house a couple of hours later." GG

A young Maine resident describes their encounter with a quadruped pale crawler humanoid. The witness has been freaked out by their experience. This report was received in September 2021:

"The crawler humanoids are real! I've been looking for answers for 2 years. What the hell was it that I saw in the woods that frightened me for life? This is not a joke! Did anyone else see this creature? I'm traumatized for life from this thing!

"It happened at my parents' house in rural Maine. I need to know what it is! How do I see it and why I'm still scared? Ok, I'm a smoker and at my parents' house, you must smoke outside. That night I could not sleep. It was around 3 AM, so I decided to go out for a smoke. When I got to the porch and turned on the light, I had a weird feeling of being watched. So, I looked. I saw 2 big orange dots. Then, before freaking out, I'm thinking it must be the reflection of the neighbor's light through the trees. Then it moves. It did the peeking move from behind the tree, back and forth 2 times. I freak the hell out when it was starting to look closer at me! I run to the patio door, trying to get the door open. But since it's an old patio door it doesn't open smoothly. I had to force it.

The 'thing' starts to run up the hill, over the train rail unto the highway. It moved incredibly fast! The path it took is not easy. It had a weird gait. Those orange eyes continued looking at me and seemed to want to get closer to me. When I got into the house I wanted to look from the large window.

I woke up my parents, not knowing what to say to them. My dad laughed at me, saying it's probably just a moose, and didn't do anything about it. This area is right beside a highway, in an area that only has 4 houses that have big distances between them. I regularly see wolves, moose, and all kinds of animals at night, so I know what it looks like! When this thing ran it made a weird sound. I don't know how to describe it!

It had long legs and arms; it ran weird on four legs! On the four legs, it still looked like it was more than 6 feet off the ground! It's so tall and fast when it runs. I was so shocked that I wanted to cry but couldn't. I was traumatized.

This is not a joke! Was it just a deformed creature? An alien? I don't know. I've never been able to sleep properly since that day. It messed me up! My mom keeps saying the dog, occasionally, just barks at night as it watches the woods. I'm not saying it's still around, but still, it freaks me out! I saw what I saw. I wish I had never gone outside for a smoke that night. I have night terrors a lot because of this. I feel like crying. I feel like it took something from me." UN

A couple noticed a pale crawler humanoid in the adjacent woods near the house. A glowing deep yellow orb was also present during this sighting. This account was received in September 2021:

"I just wanted to share my experience. Please keep in mind my experience happened 5–6 years ago now.

I spent the night at my ex's place in a very rural small town outside of New Glasgow, Nova Scotia, called Westville. We were up very late watching UFC (probably 1 am) and I went into the back bedroom of the house on the 2nd floor and happened to have glanced out the window towards the backyard.

His backyard was long and rectangular and had an embankment that sloped down to a tree line at the end of the yard which was nothing but woods from beyond that point.

When looking out the window I noticed something very pale white crawling through the tree line. It immediately caught my eye and I kept staring at it. I called my ex at the time to come in and look. We both got quiet, and we came to realize that we weren't witnessing a creature that either of us could recognize. It was human-like in form, very skinny, purely pale, and crouched forward with very long arms and would make a few movements forwards towards the yard and then back deeper into the woods again.

We had horrible phones back then at the time. I had an old Blackberry, and he was no better, and they both couldn't record what our eyes were seeing in the pitch black of night in the country. The only thing I could think of to do at this time was to call my older brother who has an interest in paranormal topics. I called him and described to him everything that we were seeing and to this day he doesn't disbelieve my accounts in any fashion. Something I said over and over to him on the phone was 'it's not moving like a human, its movements are strange' (they were almost spastic, nothing natural or orderly that I could make sense of compared to how other mammals move). It made no noise that I could hear through the window.

I was terrified but watched this thing crawl around for a solid two hours. Years later my brother found the more popular YouTube video now of the crawler in the backyard of some guy's house and he calls his preacher. That was so scarily like my experience that I got full chills, goosebumps and started to cry. It really hit me and solidified that we weren't somehow losing it or making it up, that we saw with our own eyes a crawler that night. What that man recorded is EXACTLY what I saw a few years back.

Something else that was also really messed up about my experience that I have zero explanation for. The crawler could be seen down on the left-hand side along the tree line, but we saw a glowing deep yellow orb floating between the tree line for a few moments as well. I'm wondering if there are any other accounts like this.

As I've mentioned in my story, this was an ex, so we are no longer together, so I have no idea if he continued living there or ever saw such a sight again in his backyard. I've always been curious if it's still out there and I often think about my experience as I can recall it in high detail like it was yesterday. I'll never forget what I saw until the day I die." MM

Two brothers near Tampa, Florida, encounter, at different times, a pale humanoid that they say was similar in appearance to the infamous "Dover Demon." The report was sent to me in September 2021:

"We have seen something like the Dover Demon down in Florida. On the west coast in Tampa Bay. Different climate, you know, but back then we saw it and now we live far away. But my brother saw one and I saw one too, but they weren't the same. But they were near my house there and I think they lived in the sewers.

I came home in my car and the way the road was I caught it also in the headlights. It was under the window of the room I was staying in at the time. My headlights hit it and it looked like a little kind of baby, like pink-white skin, and its arms were up like a little T-Rex like pulled in, and it was looking away from the headlights. I had to kind of drive up and around, and the way my driveway went, I had to drive around and up closer to get to the room. It was under the window! Just like all crouched down and kind of white-pink colored.

My first reaction was fear. It scared me. I was scared by it. It never hurt me, but I think I caught it off guard because of the way it was crouched. It was guarded with its arms up. (Just a note: to this day I know what it looked like. It didn't have small arms, but its arms were just pulled in).

About two years later, my little brother, who lived there at this same place, walked out to smoke a cigarette. He said that this little thing that was all hairless and bald was eating the cat food they put out for the cat under the tree, and it looked right at him and had these eyes, he said, that were just all yellow. And he also said it ran right up a tree, all weird like, and he said he turned around and went right back inside and he said it scared him too. Well, I think the Dover Demon—like thing is real and they have different types, I think, and it may be harmless, and they do scare people because of the way they look.

The one I saw under the window was like a baby kind of but not. It just looked that way, small and little and off-white. It had kind of fat legs and it was semi-seated and its arms were pulled up and its head was turned away. It was so weird. I got into that house very quickly that night. I do remember I hung up darker curtains that I pulled out of my closet. I was so wigged out.

My little brother said the one he saw was slenderer, just like the Dover Demon one, and it was weird, he said, and quick and it was eating cat food from a paper plate. He said it was a foot tall and hairless and had yellow eyes and it was way fast. And it went right up the tree. He told me he got freaked and went back in. He said he came out to smoke, and he got within ten feet of this thing before he saw it and it saw him and it was bipedal, two legs two arms, and he said it ran on two legs." PR

A young man believes that he witnessed a Gollum-like humanoid in the tree outside his bedroom window. He thought that it was eating something. The next morning, he found half-eaten field mice. This account was referred to me in October 2021:

"Alright, I swear I'm not making this up. When I lived in Texas there was this stormy night. Like, an unusually strong storm. Plenty of lightning and thunder. I had a friend over. I remember playing *Morrowind* and OG *Halo* until super late.

I was lying awake and staring out the window and listening to the rain. We had called it a night about an hour before this. There was a tree outside my window with a branch I would sometimes use to get in and out of my room. For privacy reasons. And because my parents were nosey.

In between some thunder I saw something on the branch outside. A pair of eyes, large and yellow. They just appeared where I was already staring. In a single instant, just there. A flash of light from the storm lit the tree up. It looked like freaking Gollum from LOTR. Gangly and grey with sharp teeth. Long fingers that were holding something moving. I didn't move. I didn't make a sound. It also looked like it was eating something. Then he looked right at me and smiled. A far too human smile. I screamed bloody murder. Woke the whole damn house.

Everyone told me to stop lying about stuff. You had too much caffeine before bed (I and my friend did down 2 twelve-packs of soda between us). You were asleep, it was a nightmare. I have no idea if I was seeing things, or it was a trick of the light or anything else it could have been. But I know I was awake. It was during the summertime, and I had been staying awake until sun-up for over two weeks at that point.

When I told my friend, he was skeptical, but he took my word for it. Our house was surrounded by 20 acres of woods, and we had both heard some strange sounds in those woods. When day broke and the storm let up, we went outside near my window. On the ground right under the branch were some half-eaten field mice and tails.

It has been 17 years (2004) since that day, and I still see it in my nightmares sometimes. When I think about what's out there in the dark, I remember the Gollum. Because that's what I've called it ever since." LN

An Oak Ridge, Tennessee, woman observed what she described as a red-eyed white humanoid in a local park while driving at night. The account was forwarded to me on the same night as the incident in October 2021:

"I'm going to start by saying that this is a second-hand account. I'm pissed off that I missed this, but that can't be helped. So, about three hours ago, my girlfriend left to go pick up some food. She came back about 15–20 minutes later. She was like 'I saw a monster at the park.'

At first, I didn't believe her, but after a bit of questioning, she was serious. So, we immediately got in the car (she put the food in the oven first so it wouldn't get cold) and drove over there. And there was nothing, of course. I was hoping there'd be a Halloween decoration or something, but nope. We circled the park, and then I had her park across the street so I could go look at the spot she saw it in. Nothing. I don't even know what I was thinking I'd find, but I still wanted to look around. Again, nothing. It was grass, so not like there'd be footprints anyway. And yeah, that's pretty much it, but I'll describe what she described to me.

She said she was driving, and she saw someone kind of hiding behind a tree, but poorly. Like obviously sticking out from that angle. But looking at it, she decided it wasn't a person, just kind of person shaped. She described it as white. That's what drew her attention. She said it wasn't a color she'd expect to see. And she said it had glowing red eyes. I asked her if she meant reflective like a cat, or glowing, she said glowing like a light. She described its fingers as pointy. She said it looked like it was watching the cars pass by on the street. She said it was kind of hunched over, so she couldn't be sure how tall it was, but she guessed around her height (five feet even) while in that position, probably taller fully upright. She was driving past so she said she only saw it for about 4–5 seconds.

Based on what I saw, there were two trees, maybe four feet apart, and they were maybe 30 feet from the road. I'm not great at math or measurements, so those numbers could be off. And I don't know if this is relevant or not, but we're in Oak Ridge, Tennessee. And yeah, that's it. I'd call myself a very amateur paranormal nerd. I like to watch YouTube videos and look through subs, but I'm not claiming to be anything close to an expert. I have no idea what she saw, but it sounds like a crawler is a close match. And really, I know very little about these things. I'd love to hear any thoughts or theories on this. And general information would be good too. And yeah. That's my, or at least my girlfriend's, story.

Oak Ridge isn't exactly a big city, but it is a city or at least a town. This thing was practically on the main street at 9 pm on Saturday. There are woods around here, but not anything dense enough to hide a monster in. Well maybe, I'm not exactly the woodsy type, but still, I don't think anything would fit the bill. Are they common in populated areas, or is this an unusual place to see one? I don't know how the cops would feel about me setting up cameras in a public park. Also, I don't exactly have money and cameras lying around either.

Based on the stories I've read about this thing, I'm not going to go looking for it. But investing in a solid flashlight sounds like a good idea. Hopefully, we don't see it again but never hurts to prepare.

It was seen in Alvin K Bissell Park. I'm honestly a home-body, especially with all the COVID stuff that's been going on. So maybe there's a patch of woods a few streets over I'm not aware of, but in the immediate area, I didn't see anything I'd call woods. Plus, when I looked in Google maps, it looked like it was right in the middle of the city. I don't want to go outside now. These things are like walking nightmares. Part of me wants to know more, but the rest of me is thinking there are things out there that are just better left alone." OM

I asked the couple if they would like to discuss her encounter with me by telephone. She was honestly scared that having a conversation with me would trigger some type of response by the humanoid. That is not uncommon with cryptid experiencers. Sometimes fear of retribution sets in if they report their encounter.

A British woman is driving along the A556 near her home in Norwich, Norfolk, when a light gray crawler humanoid ran across the road in front of her. I received this account in November 2021:

"I was driving home around 3 am. I was driving on the A556 near Norwich in Norfolk which is in the middle of nowhere. It's not well lit and surrounded by forest. I pretty much know this road like the back of my hand as I've been driving back and forth (mostly at night) on it for a long time. There are streetlights but they're quite dim and they don't do a great job of lighting up the road ahead.

Now as a bit of background. I'm generally a calm driver. I don't know why as I'm quite frantic in real life but when I'm behind the wheel nothing seems to faze me at all. But on that night in June 2020, I'm pretty sure I nearly had a heart attack.

I was driving along the road as per usual on my way back home. The only way to best describe this incident is to say that about 150 yards ahead of my car, out of the woods, came this humanoid creature and it bolted straight into the road.

It was a light grey colour and it was hunched over on all fours, but it could easily be about 8/9 foot tall if it stood upright. This thing bolted into the road at an unnatural speed and disappeared into the woods on the other side of the road. Now there are four lanes and no central reservation, so it was a straight sprint across.

I tried to rationalise this as a bird, but I just knew for a fact that it wasn't. Like I said before I'm a very calm driver but as soon as I saw this 'thing' I instantly turned freezing cold and started sweating, almost on the verge of crying. I don't know what my rationalization was but some part of me wanted to slam on my brakes out of panic to take a breath, but I just put my foot down and drove way too fast to get away from what I just saw.

I don't necessarily know if it's relevant, but I remember looking at the clock after it had crossed into the woods and it was dead at 03:00 am. Apparently, this is a strange hour for unexplained things to go on? If anyone else has had a similar experience or knows what the hell this thing was, I'd love to hear it because even thinking about it gives me cold chills." K

A Saskatchewan, Canada, resident describes an encounter that they had with a pale lanky humanoid crawler near their home. This incident was referred to me in November 2021:

"My great-uncle owns a lot of land in northern Saskatchewan, Canada. Some of this was pasture that he uses for cattle, but half of one of his largest properties is fenced off and the cows can't go there. In the sectioned-off lactose-free zone the entire place is densely packed with foliage. The ground itself is blotted with some small steep hills towards the entrance to the property. There is one main dirt road that goes from a Texas gate at the entrance all the way back to the farthest side of the property. Coming off the road in the hilly area we have a camp. The camp consists of an ATCO trailer.

We've always had lots of wildlife, like big cats and bears that could harm people (I had to put down a bear that came into our camp and was far too comfortable with people not too long after). I learned to recognize the sounds and sights around me and, while cautious, I'm rarely afraid of anything out there. Regardless of the seeming lack of disturbances we always were careful at night making sure to have a bright light and keep a lookout for anything.

After the first week, we began hearing noises around the camp very late at night that would drive the dog insane all night, to the point we just had to keep her inside. It almost felt like whatever it was [was] probing and checking out our camp nightly but always staying far enough away and hidden enough that we could never see it with our spotlights.

Then one night, I left my mother's camper a couple of hours after the daylight had disappeared with a lantern-style led light. I didn't have anything to defend myself (no gun, no bear spray, not even a knife) so I was a little bit more cautious and observant than usual given I felt more vulnerable. As I walked from the exit of my mom's camper, I looked around for a minute scanning the tree line. I then began the loop around to my door. I panned as I walked from right to left from the entrance to the fire pit and then to the table.

It was there, just behind the table not 20 feet away that I saw a naked extremely pale almost grey lanky humanoid figure standing still and directly facing me. As it caught my gaze, I felt my heart drop and immediately went cold. I probably only stared for 3 seconds at most, but it felt like several minutes as my brain processed what I was seeing. It stood somewhere between 6.5 and 7.5 feet tall with low slumped shoulders and had a frail thin body that reminded me of photos from the holocaust, but with disproportionately long limbs.

I ran like my life depended on it, the last few feet to my door. Once inside I grab the shotgun, stuffed several shells in my pocket, loaded the gun, aimed it at the door. I sat in silence with the hammer walked back, waiting for the doorknob to turn or the frosted glass to break. I sat and waited for hours into the early morning expecting to see or hear something, but I never did. Not even any foliage moving or items moving. Eventually around 4 AM, I lowered my guard, propped the shotgun next to my bed, and hesitantly went to sleep. When I woke up, I hardly believed what I saw the night before. I was around the area to see if there were any shapes or items that I could've mistaken and warped in my mind.

I'm not sure what I saw, but I know it wasn't human. The photos and drawings of these crawlers reminded me a great deal of it. So, I thought I'd share. Maybe one of you could enlighten me as to what it could've been doing or its intent or provide an explanation to its behaviour." G

During the current flap of winged humanoid sightings around the Chicagoland and Lake Michigan region, there have also been reports of other unknown humanoids. This report was received in September 2017:

"I'm a former Chicagoan and I was on a visit last week. I stayed a night downtown at Sofitel Chicago Magnificent Mile (20 E Chestnut St).

During the early evening, I looked out our window from the 30th floor and saw what I, at the time, assumed was a maintenance man or something on the roof of a shorter building below ours. But it moved too fluidly and disappeared too quickly for a man. It was gray and the shape I would describe as a male (with no clothes). I'd say it was about 6 ft. tall. There were no unfurled wings.

It occurred on Sunday, September 10, 2017, at approximately 7 pm CT and the thought of it hasn't left me. I couldn't see a door or anything that would allow a person to slip out of sight. It was odd to see someone/something on a roof with no rooftop features like a pool or outdoor seating, and it didn't look like there was any window-washing, construction, etc. that would easily explain why a person was on a high-rise roof and then disappear so quickly.

I told myself it was nothing and forgot about it. But on a whim, I called my friend, who'd been with me, and he told me that there have been lots of sightings of humanoids in Chicago.

I immediately panicked a bit, and I must tell you, I am very scared of things like these. I hope it doesn't mean any harm to me or anyone else. Luckily, I live in Nashville. Are these things vindictive? I'm a humble tarot reader but I don't want to cause trouble." AL

There were several instances where the witness would fear retaliation by the humanoid if they reported the sighting or encounter.

In December 2019, a witness observes a tall human-shaped being in a preserve near O'Hare International Airport. The description is interesting since it is near several other winged humanoid sighting locations. I talked to two women who observed an unknown humanoid in a forest preserve located near Rosemont, Illinois. "LJ" later forwarded the following written report:

"My friend and I were biking north on a closed Cook County Forest Preserve trail near Rosemont on December 8, 2019, at around 2 pm CT. I believe we entered the trail on the north side off Lawrence Avenue, into the Catherine Chevalier Woods. We walked our bikes at this point because the trail was muddy. It was along the Des Plaines River. Maybe a quarter mile later, the trail hooked up with a more official-looking bike trail.

After a few minutes on that trail, I was overcome with an immediate sense of anxiety and doom? About 30–50 yards away on the right side of the trail, I swear I saw something that was about 6–7 feet tall, with its back mostly toward us but slightly facing east. It looked like the back was covered in feathers or some scraggly looking light brown or gray coat. It looked kind of hunched over. I thought it was just my imagination and did not say anything to my friend about it at the time and tried to focus on a conversation we were having while biking. I felt nervous biking toward it and was not looking at it as we biked in its direction, thinking it was just my imagination. But I felt worried.

Later that day, a friend texted us jokingly to say that there were several Mothman sightings in the area we had biked through earlier that day. That's when I felt my heart sink. We didn't know much about this being before we found your site when researching the Mothman after we got back from our bike trip." LJ

The witness is a known professional in Chicago. The location is east of O'Hare International Airport. The Des Plaines

River is directly behind the convention center and hotel. I believe that this may be a key location, for whatever reason.

A group of friends in Philadelphia encounters an unexplained black humanoid while exploring the Downingtown, PA, "Twin Tunnels." Another similar incident report follows. These accounts were received in March 2021:

"I've been curious for years if anyone has ever seen the creature that crossed my path in the suburbs of Philadelphia.

I was a senior in high school, so it was 2011. My group of friends and I were always obsessed with haunted/creepy things/places. I think our interest began as kids (we lived across the street from an abandoned mental asylum that we would regularly sneak into).

So naturally when we heard about Downingtown's 'Twin Tunnels' we were psyched to go. This place is still on a driveable road, it's two attached tunnels with one active tunnel and one completely grown over with brush and water. Kind of like a swamp. They are long and curved, so there is a point in the tunnel where no light can enter, making it pitch black.

Legend has it there have been some deaths and murders there. Supposedly a pregnant woman hung herself from the middle of the tunnels, and years later in the '90s there was a woman's body chopped up and found stuffed in a suitcase, which was placed in the tunnels. So according to folklore, if you walk through the tunnels at night, you emerge from the other end with scratches on your arms. Or, if you drive through it, as we did, you could hear the feet of the suicidal pregnant woman dangling on the top of your car.

So, we go. I'm driving. We drive through a few times, park in the middle, turn the lights/car off, roll down the windows, and wait to see 'anything.' It's a bust at first, and since I'm driving, I'm ready to call it a night but a friend eagerly says one more try. So that's what we do. I park in the middle, turn the lights and car off and sit there silently waiting for something to happen. Now since this is still an active tunnel, I remind you, I have my key in the ignition ready to be turned on in an instant so that if a car comes speeding down, I can quickly turn the car on and flash the lights to let them know we're here.

So, I'm staring at the mouth of the tunnel when suddenly, I see a dark figure walk across the mouth of the tunnel. I'm amazed mind you. Almost don't believe it, until it turns into the tunnel and starts walking directly towards the car. I can only describe it as an extremely tall humanoid figure with broad shoulders, long arms that dangle almost down to its knees, and a rectangular-shaped head with no distinguishing features, just completely black. At this point, it's getting closer, and I'm so freaked out that I instinctually turned the car on, the lights flash on, and the thing vanishes. I immediately turn to my friend, and he says, 'Did you just see that?' and I reply, 'Yes.'

Although it feels nice to have another person validate what I had just seen, it has left me completely uneasy for years." JS

Here is a response to the post:

"I have had a similar experience and what I saw, I would almost describe the same! Several years ago, an old friend and I were walking on this bike trail in Northwest Arkansas. Oddly enough, she had commented how it was a 'strange night' and mentioned that she was feeling weird.

It wasn't long after, we heard what sounded like a baby crying or like a cat wailing in pain in the tree line next to the bike trail. Our first thought was that there was either an injured animal or possibly a momma cat in labor. We skimmed through the trees but found nothing. We took a few steps forward when a humanoid creature stepped out from the trees and began to cross the bike trail in front of us. It was probably close to 7 feet tall, extremely slender with knobby knees and elbows. It was all black with long arms that hung past its knees and slightly hunched. We only got the side view, but from what I could tell it had no facial features at all and it did have an odd-shaped head, but I would say more of a diamond than the rectangle that you saw. I remember its head coming to more of a point. It was so long-legged that it had walked out of the tree line, took ONE step in the middle of the bike trail, and then with the other foot, he had reached the other side and disappeared into a fence.

The girl I was with looked at me panicked and said, 'What do we do?' Because at this point, it [was] continue past the creature or turn around and run back past whatever was wailing in the trees. I ended up saying, 'RUN!' And we turned around and did not stop running until we ended up back at our apartment slamming the door behind us.

I went back the next morning because the way it vanished into the fence almost seemed as though there had to have been a hole in it the creature walked through. But when I went back it was nothing but solid fence the whole way down. No sign of anything from the night before." AD

This phenomenon of corporeal black or dark humanoids has surfaced more often since the recent advent of pale humanoid/crawler encounters. Are these black disappearing beings related to the white humanoids? Considering the legends associated with the tunnel location, could this have been a thought-form manifestation? Some people may pass these off as ghost stories or shadow men. I don't think that is the case in some of these encounters.

A wild boar hunter in the US Southwest was out at night testing and sighting his new scope when he spots a humanlike figure in the darkness. He soon realizes this was not a man, but something much different. This account was forwarded to me in September 2021:

"I enjoy hunting wild boar, though I have been deer hunting and have been known to get a turkey for Thanksgiving. For those of you that don't know, boar is a big problem in the United States. A sow can have two litters a year and it's not uncommon for a litter to consist of 10 or more pigs. Given that pigs eat anything and everything it's not hard to see why the game commissions make it legal to hunt them with almost no restrictions. In my state, it's illegal to hunt most large mammals with night vision scopes, except for boar and coyote.

I took it to a range and sighted it in. There was an area that was peppered with boar activity that I knew would be perfect for a night hunt. It was easily accessible with my truck with easy-to-find spots that I could set up in that overlooked a large easy to navigate clearing. The night started uneventful, mostly me tinkering with my new toy, cycling through the settings. I was a little impatient, I'd spotted multiple deer, but they were out of season, and as I mentioned earlier, my current setup wasn't legal for deer. I moved to another spot I'd seen days earlier that probably wasn't much better than my first, but it gave me something to do and a new angle to look around with my new scope.

After an hour or so of glassing the area, it dawned on me. This spot doesn't have much animal activity at all, no rabbit or owls, the deer that I'd seen were hundreds of yards from where I was. Why was this pocket of land so dead at night but lively in the day? I'd set up around 10 pm and it was about 2 am when I started to think about packing up, maybe setting up a target before I left. I heard a crunch come from the direction I came from before. I panned my scope over and saw the silhouette of a small bear. It's important to note that my scope isn't exactly 'night vision.' It's a thermal scope, kind of like a black and white version.

I adjusted my range and zoomed in a little. I remember jolting a little when I saw that it wasn't really a bear, it was a man. Because he was so low and hunched over, I thought I was looking at a young bear. Is that a game warden? It couldn't be. I would've seen the headlights coming up the road from where I was perched. And where could he have walked from? I was 30 miles away from anything and on public lands. I was about to call out when I noticed he was naked. No shoes, pants, or anything. I remember being disturbed by his movements, like a squirrel or something. Twitchy and grabbing at the foliage, sniffing around, and palming the tree.

Was that my tree? The one I'd been leaning against earlier? The thought terrified me, could he smell me? Then he did something I still have nightmares about today. He squatted and placed his hands in the dirt between his feet and stared straight up like a dog mid howl. And I heard it, a voice coming from that direction, a female voice. 'Help! I'm lost!' There was a long pause but neither of us moved a muscle. The center of my sights was trained at the dirt in front of his feet, I couldn't bring myself to aim directly at another person. Were they lost? Was this some guy that had gone crazy out here? Why was his voice so feminine? 'Help! Please! I can't walk!' the voice called out. That's when I called BS. Not only could he walk, when I first saw him, he was traversing the land with ease for a naked person, so good I mistook him for a bear.

That's a trap! This guy is trying to lure me to him with a damsel in distress routine. Luckily the lack of activity before had caused me to pack up most of my gear. I think I may have left behind a hat and a sitting pad, but I didn't care at that moment. I took my eyes off him for a moment to get my pack on. I buckled my chest strap and scrambled for my rifle. To my horror, he was in the same position, but his face was staring in my direction, and I swear I saw a smile. How the hell had he heard me get up and put my gear on? He must've easily been 150 yards away. 'F off!' I screamed in that direction. He stood upright and it hit me how tall and skinny he was. Easily six feet and very lean. He took a couple of long strides in my direction, and I instinctively sent a round sailing above his head into the tree line. He was freaky as hell, but he hadn't really threatened me, what would I tell the cops?

He stopped dead in his tracks and hunched down on all fours. 'The next one is meant for you! Go away!' He stayed on all fours and this time I had my sights on the center of him. His eyes were just above the grass like a large cat or something. I was trying to stop my trembling and knew that my voice had cracked a little on that last warning. I was terrified. That standoff probably only lasted a minute or two, maybe less, but it felt like forever. In an instant, he bolted left towards the tree line opposite the road. So much for not being able to walk. I couldn't keep him in my scope he was moving so fast. He disappeared into the brush, and I sent another round sailing high in his direction. I racked another round and tried to pocket that mag and swap for a fresh one, but I dropped it and didn't bother looking for it. I wasn't far from my truck, and I wanted to get out of there.

I could hear him in the distance, yelling in this weird

sound that could have been a laugh or a cry. I scrambled up the trail and arrived at my truck breathless. I tossed my gear into the cab but kept the rifle in the passenger seat and sped off.

For the longest time, I said that story from the perspective of having spotted some deranged crackhead living off the land like some kind of caveman. I reported it to fish and game but all they did was scold me for hunting at night alone, and I never received an update. It wasn't until I told this story at a camping trip that my nephew told me about rakes and pale crawler humanoids. My story scared the piss out of him because the spot we were camping was technically the same forest I'd seen this thing. Just 50 miles east of it.

He was so spooked his mom (my cousin) had to take him home. She was really pissed. I've gone down the rabbit hole. I'm not saying what I saw was a crawler humanoid. I'm saying that if such a thing exists, I may have dodged quite the bullet that night." PC

In February 2016, I received an inquiry from an elderly woman in the Phoenix suburb of Surprise, Arizona. She witnessed two humanoid beings standing outside her bedroom window a few days before Christmas 2015. The following report includes most of the information from the incident, though there are a few personal notes that I have redacted. I called and talked to the witness soon after receiving the report to gather more details. The witness was extremely alarmed by the incident and was desperately seeking answers.

Here is the initial email:

"Hello Mr. Strickler, Feb. 10, 2016

Around 12-21 or 12-22-2015, I woke up at about 1:30 am. I glanced out my bedroom window, and this is what I saw: Two short gray people-like figures with coneheads. The tallest stood there at approximately 4 feet tall, and the smallest one, about 3 feet in height, stood directly in front of the taller one. They just stood motionless. I looked, then looked again, as I have never seen anything like this EVER! I set on the edge of my bed, and I just kept looking at them. They didn't move. Neither one of them had facial features at all. It appeared to me they had something over their heads to hide their appearance. I didn't let my dog out, as I didn't know what could happen. I lay back down in bed. I went to sleep. I didn't wake until the next morning at 8:30 am?

I called the police a week or so later. They just told me to go to the ER or to call the Crisis Center. About a week later I went to my church. The priest didn't believe me or didn't want to discuss this encounter. I have done a lot of research online, and these coneheads have been seen before, and are described as I have described them. I have never believed in the paranormal, or have I ever viewed any website on my computer until after I encountered these 2 Grey little people looking into my bedroom window.

This was not a dream. I was completely awake. No medicine I take has any side effects that would cause me to hallucinate! I am a senior citizen; I am living alone. This has scared me. They have not come back. I worry that they might come back. I have so many questions. I also called CH 113 EWTN TV. The person I talked to at EWTN didn't believe me and did not want to discuss the matter. Please e-mail me. I have not told my friends or family. Please help me with the answers I have. I pray daily that I never see them again!"
Name withheld.

I called the witness and received more specific details. She did state that these beings wore full-length cloaks that were the same color (grayish) as the cone-like head. She also stated that she never sleeps more than three hours without waking, but she slept for an uninterrupted seven hours after the sighting, which she states she has never done before or since.

Rendering of the humanoid the witness described.

A group of friends was camping out on the Montour Trail in western Pennsylvania. One of the friends encounters an eight-to-nine-foot-tall unknown humanoid while gathering wood. The following account was forwarded to me by a second party in May 2020:

"At the time of writing this, I am living in western Pennsylvania, a little south of Pittsburgh. I was in Boy Scouts for most of my life, so I feel very comfortable in the woods and go camping often. Upon hearing Governor Wolf's school closure plan, I decided that it was time for some cold weather camping. It was March, it wasn't that cold, but it did drop to 40 degrees at night, and the people who I went with weren't avid campers. If you're from Pittsburgh you may know the Boggs campsite on the Montour Trail in Allegheny County, Pennsylvania. That's where we went. They, of course, only brought alcohol and didn't bring any sleeping bags, blankets, or pillows. So naturally, I assumed they were going to sit by the fire all night.

It was light when we first got there, and the fire pit was still smoldering. We used the coals from the previous camper's fire to light ours and immediately I knew that I would have to provide wood for the fire until I went to bed. They passed out beer at around 3 pm and after having 2–3 beers I just wanted dinner. So, we made some food and ate. By this time, it would have had to have been close to 5 pm and it started to rain a little bit, as was forecasted. So, we took shelter in a small building that was on-site and occasionally one of them would throw some wood on the fire.

After a while of just hanging out, they asked if I had any blankets. I always have blankets. Nothing special but we've had some bad snowstorms in the past and a couple of scratchy car blankets are always useful. They each got a blanket except for 'R,' as we'll call him, who got my summer sleeping bag that I brought just in case.

By now it was dark, 9–9:30 pm, and the fire was getting low. I start off to find some more wood. I return with the wood and just kind of hang out and talk and listen to music. Eventually the fire, again, dies down a little bit, and, again, it's my job to get more wood. Because we had been there for a while and there were people there before us most of the wood near the shelter was either small or all used up, so I had to keep going farther and farther away from camp to find wood. It was 12:30 am, and close to 50 degrees still so we're all doing well. I have a flashlight, a nice one that I use for scuba diving, that is kind of bright, so I use it on the low setting on land.

At this point, I'm far enough away from camp that my friends can't really see me. There's like an embankment between the Montour Trail and someone's driveway that you must cross to get to more woods. But I'm comfortable alone because I knew what I was doing, and they could hear me if I needed them.

I start to hear a weird whistling sound, kind of like someone inhaling through a snorkel, but I chalk it up to the wind. The air was starting to get kind of cold, so I just took back what I had and put some on the fire. I have on 2 long sleeve shirts and an Army surplus coat that is super warm, but my friends are in windbreakers and hoodies and, oh yeah, it's raining. Off to get more wood.

This time I started taking into consideration the type of wood that I would collect. There was a lot of pine but that burns fast which is why I had to go collect it so often. The stretch of woods near the driveway was pretty much all pine, a few maples but nothing big. So, I keep walking knowing that this area has both conifers and deciduous trees near each other. As I'm wandering and collecting wood, I notice that the rain has turned to fine snow. Time to head back just in case it picks up.

Then the whistling started again, a lot louder now. Ok, weird. There isn't any more wind than there was before. Maybe it changed directions. I keep walking. By now I can hear the music from camp and pick up the pace a little bit. Just as I summit the embankment and prepare to clamber down the other side [a] LOUD noise echoes behind me. Did a tree fall? Shining my flashlight around I couldn't see any signs that that was the case and didn't see any source. In my head, it doesn't matter because I'm back at camp anyways and I can try the marsh behind our shelter next time.

They were getting cold. The temperature dropped to around 30 degrees and the wind and snow had picked up. Car blankets helped the boys a little bit, but they couldn't go to sleep in the tent that I brought without freezing, except for 'R' who slept like a rock all night after about 3:30 am. We decide to finish off the last beers.

It's about 4:30 am. I'm about ready for bed at this point because I was tired. I offer to go collect more wood before I retire to my sleeping bag and cot (I camp comfy when I don't have to carry it far) and they said they would join me. We split up and I end up heading back to where I was before, except this time I left my flashlight on high, and I made a bunch of noise to scare off that deer or whatever that was there earlier.

I end up a little further away from the camp. Then the whistling starts again. This time I could tell the direction it was coming from, my left, and shined my flashlight around that area before just returning to collecting wood. Then the sound stops briefly, then picks up again in a different direction less than a minute later. This time in front of me and a little to the right, back into the pines. Maybe the branches of certain trees catch the wind just right and make the noise, I think, 'Whatever,' and move on. Then on my way back, the noise was following me, darting from left to right but always like right behind me. I don't see anything whatsoever. Then the noise makes like one sharp whistle and pauses, then I hear it, 'Damn it's cold out here.'

It was 'R', but I couldn't find him with my flashlight, so I called, 'Where you at?' It sounded like he turned around because I heard a branch snap and a bit of movement. I pointed my flashlight at where the sound was coming from, and I didn't see 'R' anywhere. Maybe he's behind a bush or a tree or something. I call out again, 'R?' No reply this time. He might be lost or something because we weren't at camp, and he saw my flashlight moving so he came to look. 'R, where are you?' Nothing. Then, louder. 'I'm going back to camp,' because I thought he was trying to scare me. Shining my flashlight around one last time I spot something diving into a bush about 40 feet from where I had heard 'R' turn around. 'I see you, man. Grab some wood and come back.' He's 6' and 230–250 lbs. I shine the light around for a few more seconds then turn around again and start walking.

The whistling is back. No matter what speed I moved at it always seemed the same distance away. I decided that I'd just kind of sit under a tree and wait for 'R' to pass by because he had to come back sometime, right? I wanted to save the battery of my flashlight so I turned it off and closed one eye, so it would adjust faster. By now the snow had picked up a good bit, which is another reason to stop, in case 'R' got lost. I couldn't really see far because there was a lot of cloud cover despite it being a full moon. The whistling never got closer, but it did start to move around a little bit, in a really odd circle. It would start in one spot, stop, then promptly start in another spot that was in a different direction. I realized that it had to be the wind or something because it was moving super-fast and was moving at random. Now where the hell is 'R'? I turn on my flashlight between whistles and call out again, 'R!' It's important to note here that the whistling never picked up while I looked around. It normally only stopped for a second or two. It was very quiet.

There was now 3 inches of snow on the ground so maybe

that muffled it? Anyways, upon not hearing 'R' I thought that maybe I missed him or didn't hear him at all and started to head back to camp. As I stood up and brushed the dirt off my ass, I shined the flashlight around one more time. I was thinking in my head, 'I definitely heard him.' After I stood up with the wood in my arms and began to walk back towards camp, I saw something move out of the corner of my eye. My flashlight, being a diving light, has a wrist mount that I was wearing so I could use it and carry things. I turned towards and scanned the area. Nothing. Not even 4 steps more and I saw another movement. Now the whistling was back. Damn, that gets annoying. The flashlight was on low so I could see maybe 40 feet around me and didn't see anything, but I knew it was time to pick up the pace.

Now the whistling was followed by flashes of movement. Great, it's not the wind. At this point I'm speed walking, being tall I can move quickly if I must, and I was definitely traveling at jogging speed. 'R,' a lumbering beast when he runs, could not move this fast or this quietly through the woods. I decided to turn off the flashlight and move into some brush that was close by. Not sure why but I was getting a little freaked out and had the shakes even though I was warm. It was silent again. What is it? Is it hunting me? Coyote? Not a coyote.

There was a long period of silence, then there was whistling. This time it wasn't doing circles around me, it was just moving around where I had turned off the flashlight. My eyes adjusted and I peeked out from under the bush that I was rolled up under. Nothing, just that damned whistling. I waited for a little while and just kind of looked around. Then I heard it speak.

In a really gargled impression of me, it called out, 'Big man.' It took everything I had not to panic. Not 'R,' not human, not a deer, not the wind. Then it spoke again, cutting off strangely like you just lifted the needle off of a record but picking back up again with 'back to camp' still in my voice. MY DAMN VOICE! I normally don't like hearing recordings of myself anyways but now I REALLY don't like them. It said a few more things, in different voices that I didn't recognize. All the voices were either talking about how cold it was or questions like 'what was that?' and 'stop screwing with me,' but they all seemed like whoever was talking had something built up in their throat.

Then it went quiet. I poked my head out of the bushes again and saw something sitting against a tree in the same position I had been in. Left leg straight out, right leg at an angle, hands behind my head. It could have fooled me as being 'R.' We both kind of sit the same way except his ADHD usually makes him fidget with his hands. OK, so who's sitting in the woods with me. I lay there, silent, and just watch. It begins to whistle. Ah, so that's where that was coming from. It moves its hand around in a fist out in front of it, the same way that I look around with my flashlight, and then it started to stand up. Damn, it's tall. I only weigh 166, skin and bone mostly, so when I say that this thing was skinny don't take it lightly. I could see how thin its long spindly arms were silhouetted against the snow that coated a bush behind it. When it stood up it was hunched over. It walked a few paces away from the tree and stood up the whole way. I was shocked!

I worked with backdrops for theater productions and the walls we use the most are around 8 feet high, and this thing would have easily been able to see over one. I'm talking by at least a foot higher. It slowly peered around, no hair on its head and its side profile showed a very disfigured skull. The jaw hung far down and there weren't really lips that stuck out, but it was hard to tell because of how dark it was. It let out one final 'R? Big man?' Kind of like someone with Tourette's would say it because they were just random words that it strung together. Then it SCREAMED!

My dad used to take me to airshows a lot as a kid and this must have been the same pitch and volume as an F-16. I couldn't move. It peered around, head just seemingly sweeping the area. Then it crouches down and leaps for a tree with the lowest branch being around 10–15 feet and lands feet first on one of the branches and sits there, squatting, whistling, and just staring around. Then it takes off. Faster than should be allowed in nature. I count to ten in my head. The forest sleeps. I slowly make my way out from under the bush and begin to creep back towards camp, this time avoiding using my flashlight or making any noise if possible. I climb the embankment and take one last look towards the woods, unsure if that just happened or if I was asleep. I tumble down the other side of the embankment and return to the relative safety of the big fire with 'Y' and 'J,' the other two who went for wood.

'Where's your wood?' asks 'Y.' 'Oh it, uh, had bugs.' 'It's fine, we got a lot anyways.' They stacked up a solid pile of oak and pine, not enough for the night but enough for a little while at least. 'Where's R?' I ask warily. 'Check the tent.' There he was passed out snoring the way he always does. Well, ok then. I climbed into my sleeping bag to warm up a little bit because I was covered in snow when I got back.

Then I heard it scream again! Oh, please don't tell me it's coming here. The other two looked at me wide-eyed. Normally, if I recognize a sound, I say what it is out loud, so they know what's up. I had no response. They asked if I heard the first one. Good, they heard it too. I answered with a nod as I unlocked the car in case we needed to book it. They asked if I saw it. Nod. What was it? No freaking clue. I described it to them quietly so that I could listen for more noises, and I told them about it imitating my voice. 'Y' was pretty freaked out. 'J' thought I was BSing him and said it was [an] owl. I got out of my sleeping bag, threw my coat back on and joined them at the fire.

For the first time in a while, I looked at my phone. 5:45 am. We looked up native owl calls and came up empty-handed. The same with every other animal we tried. 'J' seemed a little nervous. 'Y' suggested that 'maybe it's a truck on the highway.' 'Yeah, that's probably it,' I replied blankly, and 'J' gave me a look that said that he knew it probably wasn't. They didn't sleep. I forced sleep upon myself since I had to drive the car home.

The next morning, we went for a walk. It didn't snow much after I got back so you could kind of follow my footprints. The tree the thing leaped onto was out of reach of me on J's shoulders. 'R' was still asleep, but I think I might have been able to reach it if I was on his shoulders. The tree I sat under had scratch marks on it. I think they're from deer shedding the velvet off their antlers, but it creeped me out, nonetheless. The tree it sat under had footprints EVERYWHERE. There seemed to be no order to them at all. It was amazing. It looked like it had run over every square inch of that area, coming as close to the bush I was in.

I don't really know much about cryptids or anything. I'd appreciate some feedback." JD

I talked to JD and sent an investigator to the location. Since the snow was gone, there wasn't much evidence to gather. Mimicking is another characteristic that is sometimes reported by witnesses. JD seemed very forthright and emotional during our conversation. He did mention "Rake" and "Wendigo" to me, so I know that he had been conducting research. I believe that he was honestly fearful during the encounter. One of his friends, "J," did offer a brief written statement confirming the screams.

A short video was recorded by a Poland farmer, who had apparently been hearing snarling sounds emanating from the woods near his property. I ran the video through the CGI detecting software, and there seems to be no deception digitally. I captured several screenshots from the video and present them for your assessment. The video was posted on YouTube in December 2020.

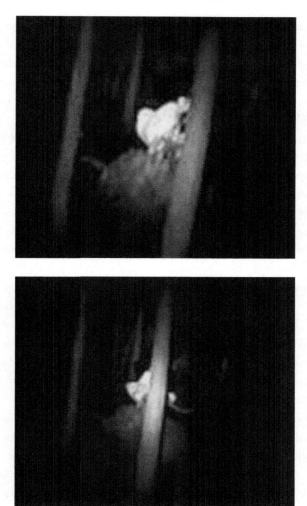

The next account was told to me in the third person, and it's quite bizarre. A deer hunter, sitting in a tree stand near Dublin, Virginia, is startled by scratching sounds directly below him. For hours he attempts to catch a glimpse of this unknown being. The account was received in September 2020:

"This story was told to me by my wife, and it happened to one of her friends. I didn't get to hear it first-hand. The man this happened to is a large no-nonsense security guard. A quiet dude who likes to joke and isn't dramatic. My wife tells me that it's weird for him to tell a story and not have it end with a punchline.

"So early November 2010, somewhere near Dublin, Virginia, Paul was walking through the woods toward his tree-stand. It was deer season and rifle in hand on that crisp early Saturday morning he was ready to ambush some game. He excitedly arrived at the tree stand and took a seat at the top. Paul settled in and got comfortable. The only sounds he could hear were leaves scattering as they were blown around in the wind. That morning, it was still. In his words, 'it was damn peaceful.' After a time, he fell asleep.

"Paul jerked awake at the sound of scratching at the base of his tree. He said it was like a large cat or bear was stretching against the tree putting its weight forward and scraping the bark off to mark its territory. Maybe a black bear or even a cougar. No way it was a deer though and whatever it was, it was standing directly under him. He leaned over the tree-stand, trying to see what it was. As he did it rushed away in the opposite direction and went behind the tree, just out of sight, leaves loudly crunching under its feet as it went.

"Paul waited to see what it would do, gun ready. If it was a bear, it might try to climb up the tree and he might have to shoot it. He thought it might be easiest to scare it off before it got aggressive. He aimed his gun up and fired a warning shot. The blast echoed over the forest, and everything became still again. He didn't describe it as being peaceful this time. This time called it 'downright eerie.'

"Nothing climbed up the tree as he had feared but nothing ran from behind the tree as he had hoped. Nothing moved at all. Just leaves swirling around in the wind. Paul began to wonder if it was a person instead of an animal. Maybe someone who was trying to play a trick on him but was too scared of being shot to move now.

"He shouted, 'HEY!' No response. He shouted again, 'Come out. Say something. I don't want to shoot you, but I will if you don't say anything.' Again nothing. He waited and thought animals don't stay still for this long and it might be safe to come down. Paul slowly stood up and stepped onto the crude wooden step nailed on the side of the tree. As his foot touched the step, he heard something move around to the other side of the tree. Paul scrambled around the tree stand and tried to look and see what it was, almost dropping his rifle as he went. Again, it was gone before he could catch a glimpse, back behind the tree.

"Paul stood next to his seat and readied his rifle. Was this person or animal dangerous? Maybe a rabid animal or mentally sick human? An escaped prisoner?

"He decided that being afraid was not the best thing to do in this situation and instead of panicking, Paul waited. Unfortunately, the other thing was as patient as him and it waited too. Neither moved as the sun changed position and afternoon changed to dusk. Paul realized he had to relieve himself and if there was going to be a struggle, he could at least choose not to have it in darkness.

"Paul stood and stepped onto the ladder again and again the other thing scrambled around to the other side of the tree. He froze for a moment and then steadied himself and climbed down quickly, stumbling at the bottom, trying to ready his weapon, pointing it out, holding it tight against his shoulder. He walked backward stepping through the leaves and he could hear it moving like it was trying to stay hidden. Paul circled the tree until he was standing under the tree-stand, and he noticed the scratches. Running parallel six deep gashes in the tree (two sets of three).

"As he was looking at the marks left by the other thing, he saw a red arm. No mistake that it was a man. A red man. Paul was clear on this 'I don't mean it was a red man like a Native American Indian, I mean he was red like a stop sign. Like the devil is red.'

"Paul lowered his gun and stepped backward and as he did the red man stepped out from behind the tree. He was completely naked and smiling huge, his teeth showing white the size of baseball cards in crooked patterns. His eyes were vacant and menacing. The red man never blinked as he stared. (Paul didn't describe what his body looked like or offer a reason why this red-skinned man was naked.)

"Paul took a step forward and as he did the red man mirrored his action exactly. Paul shook and stepped back. The red man froze as he did but moved forward as Paul moved backward. Paul raised his gun and pointed at the red man. 'Stay back,' he shouted. The red man began to walk toward him. Paul scrambled backward. He wasn't prepared to shoot, not at another person.

"Paul stepped back and slung his rifle over his shoulder, began to run back in the direction of his truck. His feet quickly carried him. He glanced over his shoulder and saw that the red man was just standing there. Staring at him. He slowed down and watched the red man shrink as he moved away from him. Smiling and naked. Staring. Paul lost sight of him a moment later and it was dark by the time he reached his truck. He said, 'Sometimes I lay awake worrying if I'll see the red man again. Whoever he was, he let me go.'

"He hasn't repeated the story since." SS

A group of friends in Ardara, Pennsylvania, encounters a

very pale upright humanoid standing on the railroad track. One of the friends describes it as being like the "Slender Man." The account was referred to me in December 2021:

"One day in March of my sophomore year in high school (2014) I had 2 friends of mine sleep over on a Friday night. These 2 friends and I were always adventurous and getting ourselves in something we had no business doing at 15/16 years old, but we did it anyway. So, we have the sleepover and do whatever Friday.

We wake up early on Saturday morning somewhere between 7 and 8 am. My parents ALWAYS slept in on Saturday mornings. My mom, being a bus driver and out of the house before I was even up for school, and my dad working 9–5 in the back of a car dealership. I, knowing my parents have at least another 3 hours of good solid sleep, say, "Hey, let's go to the train tracks and smoke our cigarettes and hit this weed we have." We easily could have gone on my back deck or somewhere a little closer but what fun would that have been. We get all our stuff and head out very early.

The train tracks aren't a very long distance from my house, about an 8-minute walk. I lived in a small neighborhood; it is called the village of Ardara. No more than 30 houses in the small town that is located to the side of a drag called Rt. 993. My mom always said, "If you blink, you'll miss it," (where we live). We walk the shoulder of 993 for maybe 50 feet and there is a post office for Ardara and right across from this post office is a bridge to go onto Leger Road. We go over the bridge, which has been shut down for years, and once you cross the bridge there is a little cut in the woods that loops you back around to the train tracks. The train tracks where I was are a very long and straight track. You could see at least a mile down. And on each side of the train track is a very steep hillside. At this point (March) there was no greenery on shrubs/trees/bushes. You could very visibly see anything on these hillsides. For example, a deer would not be able to hide well. My friends and I are on the train tracks, and we walk down them maybe half a football field in distance. We stop and huddle up ready to light our half bowl of weed.

Slenderman

This is where things get spooky. As we huddle to light up our bowl, I, knowing these train tracks, glance one time back to

make sure a train is not coming thru the straightaway. At the moment of checking that's when I say out loud, 'Do you guys see that too?' And I ask this to make sure I am not seeing things. They both say faintly, 'Yes.' What I saw is just downright unexplainable. I will try my best to describe it.

It wasn't a man, but it was the same height and body stock of a man. This thing had no face, no ears, no mouth, no hair, no hat on, no eyes, no nose. This thing didn't have a skin tone. It was white. It was the whitest thing I have ever [seen] 'skin' wise. It had an outfit very relatable to [the] 'Michael Myers' character. Like a blue jumpsuit that you would see on a janitor or an auto mechanic. It was also relatable to 'Slender Man.' But it wasn't tall and abnormal like Slender Man. Just the whole white face no facial feature thing. This 'man' was standing facing us about 25 yards away. We just walked down here and were walking toward where he would have been. It appeared out of nowhere. Literally.

When my friends both say, 'Yes, we see this,' I run [in] the other direction back towards the bridge as fast as I can. I look back at them one time just to make sure they are okay. They are both behind me. When I looked back, I saw the thing. It was at the same place it was before, the only thing that changed was that it wasn't positioned facing us and the bridge. Its body was now facing the hillside and looking directly forward. We run back under the bridge and up the little cut back to on top of it. It took us probably no more than 15 seconds to get back to the bridge. We stood there for at least an hour. We waited. We waited so patiently to see something, or someone walk around or just anything. Nothing ever happened.

I have told my brother, my mom, co-workers, and friends. Everyone believes me but no one ever has any kind of reasoning or anything for what happened. I remember it so vividly and it still scares me to this day. I can't explain what happened. Does anyone have any input?

I am from Pennsylvania and like I said lived in the village of Adara, Westmoreland County. You can easily look up the Ardara post office and see the bridge across from it. There are even some pictures I've found of a train enthusiast that has pictures below and on the bridge." HC

I know a few colleagues and investigators in Westmoreland County, PA, so I presented this account to them. I was somewhat surprised by two of the responses. It seems that other witnesses have seen a pale humanoid figure in the area over the past decade. I asked if the term "Slender Man" was ever associated with the sightings, which didn't register with these investigators. I was told, though, that the known sighting witnesses are residents of Adara who are well respected within the community. The previous sightings, as far as they can determine, did not take place on the railroad tracks.

Is it possible that the Adara, PA, pale humanoid could be a thought-form manifestation? I'm not sure if these sightings have reached the level of "urban legend," but I do believe that there is potential for this phenomenon to occur in similar circumstances.

5

A CAUTIONARY TALE

A young man embarks on a rite of passage at his father's insistence. The ordeal may be an embellished account, but an interesting, yet cautious tale, nonetheless. The account was forwarded to me in December 2020:

"In the early days of February, just before my senior year, I was prompted by my father to undertake a 'rite of passage' as he called it. I was to be left alone to fend for myself in a section of Tennessee's Cherokee National Forest for three days and two nights.

I was against the trip from the beginning. Sure, I liked hunting and camping, but this was extreme, too extreme for my tastes. But it was tradition; passed down from father to son in my family for generations. Who was I to break tradition?

So, against my reservations, and against the feeling that this was a stupid idea, I packed up my backpack, grabbed my .30-06 bolt action rifle, and climbed into the cab of my dad's pickup.

It was a long drive. I was a little pissed that my dad was

basically forcing this on me, and our uneasy silence only made the hours feel like days. We only stopped once at a gas station about ten miles from our cabin. It was fifteen miles of dirt to my dad's cabin that his grandfather had left him, which would, in turn, be left to me. It was tradition, after all.

But I wouldn't be getting the luxury of a cabin, no. We were parking the truck, and my father was driving me up deeper into the woods on a four-wheeler to a random, undisclosed point. I would then have three days to find my way back. If I succeeded, I'd become a man in my dad's eyes, and we'd also be getting a new swimming pool for the summer. It was bribery, but I would be going into my senior year in August and having a big pool would cement my popularity. It was vain, and I was doing this for mostly selfish reasons, but I also wanted to make my dad proud.

I stepped out of the toasty truck to the calm, frigid forest air. The cabin was a small two-story log affair, worn from age, but well maintained. A new wooden wraparound porch had been built last summer and needed staining that we'd never gotten around to, but otherwise, the cabin was pristine.

It was a tremendously peaceful place, far removed from the troubles of civilization, and I felt like I was intruding on hallowed ground. I brushed off the shiver that clawed down my spine and buttoned my long coat to my neck. Immediately most of the chill went away, and I shook off my unease.

Before I could take a step to the cabin, my dad came around the front of the truck and held out his hand. 'Thomas, hand me your bag,' he demanded, in a curt, no-nonsense tone. As he told me to hand him my backpack, I did so without question, and he immediately went inside, telling me to wait on the porch. I marched across the wood and sat in the rocking chair while my dad bustled around inside.

'I loaded everything you'll need for three days in the bag.

You have a couple of days of food, but it's only for an emergency. I also added a flare gun for an actual emergency.'

He handed me back the bag, and it was stuffed full, a lot had been added to it, so much that string strained against the nylon fabric. I hefted it onto my shoulder, and though it was much heavier than before, it wasn't cumbersome. I could carry it all day and I didn't think it would bother me.

After he handed me the pack, we unloaded the four-wheeler from the back of his truck, and we set off up the small walking trail next to the house. From memory, the path went on for dozens of miles and followed the stream as it snaked through the wilderness.

We rode until the dirt road ended and humanity fell away to the deep woods. The ride got bumpy as we wound around trees and over small rocks and for a minute, I was afraid of hazards. My dad was an experienced outdoorsman, though, and knew these woods well. A few hours later, we'd reached the destination.

It was a small clearing nestled under a copse of trees, the remains of a previous campsite, long since put out, rested in the center of the dirt surrounded by a circle of rocks.

'I was up here scouting a couple of weeks ago, so I know the route I'd take to get back,' he said cheekily. 'Be careful, son. And call me if there's an emergency. I'm only a few hours away and I should be able to see the flare if there's trouble.'

'Yeah, because I'll be able to get a signal out here,' I replied, holding up my now useless phone.

'Well, there's always the flare gun, but I'm confident you'll be fine, and besides, the flare's only there if you decide to give up,' he said, laughing.

With a parting wave, he departed, rolling back down the

mountain and leaving me stranded in the woods for three days.

The first thing I did was take inventory and catalog my belongings. I undid the pack and carefully emptied its contents onto the ground.

I had a pair of long johns, some extra socks, and underwear. A box of matches, a hunting knife, and a miniature shovel. A Ziploc bag filled with a blend of spices, a canteen of water, two days of vacuum-sealed rations and water pouches, and the flare gun. Along with my hammock and blanket.

I had everything I needed to make camp and survive if my hunting skills proved to be lacking. I had over thirty miles of wilderness to hack through before I hit the main roads and could circle back to the cabin. Dad told me it should take me at least two days, three if I didn't get lucky with my hunts.

I had a few hours to kill before nightfall, and I wanted to get some miles in and find my bearings. The best bet, I thought, would be to hike along the stream until it ended. It was somewhat close to the trail, but not on it, as that would be cheating, but it would give me an excellent landmark to keep me oriented. So, with mild hesitation, I packed up and set off through the woods.

I would have to hunt before it got dark if I didn't want to go hungry, and I only had an hour or two before the light fell enough to make hunting impossible. After searching around for about ten minutes, I found a good spot to set up camp for the evening, and I dropped my bag and grabbed my rifle, chambered a cartridge, and double-checked the safety. My game was rabbit since I didn't have the tools needed to string up and gut a deer.

I set off and crept through the brush, looking for signs of a nearby den. Rabbits are most active at dawn or dusk, so it was the perfect time to hunt them. Less than five minutes later, I found signs of rabbit trails in the underbrush a few hundred yards from camp; I leaned against the tree, just waiting.

The rabbit I wanted appeared half an hour later, hopping out of the brush without a care in the world. It was a plump eastern cottontail. It stopped and sniffed, giving me my opening. The crack of my rifle pierced the air and the cottontail dropped dead. I'd hit my mark, taking it in the neck to not spoil any of the meat. It was a decent-sized rabbit, more than enough for dinner. I bagged it and went back to camp.

When the meat was cleaned, I rubbed some spices into the meat to remove some of the game taste and skewered it with a stick I'd sharpened.

I wasn't the best cook and didn't have the right tools and ingredients, so the meat was a little dry and bland, but filled me up nicely, and I washed it down with a swig from my canteen. I even had leftovers. I wrapped them up in cloth and sat them by the fire, ready to be eaten for breakfast in the morning.

With nothing else to do for the evening and night had fallen an hour ago, I decided to turn in for the evening and get an early start in the morning. I had many miles to cover, and I would have to hunt again at some point the next day for dinner.

In the morning, I woke up refreshed from one of the best nights of sleep I'd ever had and was eager to take on the day. I was in such a good mood that it took me a few minutes to realize something was off.

In the middle of packing up my hammock and gathering my supplies, I couldn't help but notice that the leftover rabbit was missing from next to the fire. I searched around for it in vain, thinking the wind might have caught it and blown it away from the camp. But there was nothing.

I chalked it up to a wild animal, but that unsettled me.

Deer didn't often eat meat, and I didn't think a deer would get anywhere near my campsite. The smoke from the embers of the fire would have been enough to keep most animals away.

Black bears were common enough in the forest, but they should still be hibernating during this time of year. Right now, there wasn't anything larger than a deer in these woods, so unless it was a coyote, it had to have been a deer. But there were no tracks anywhere around my campsite, so no answers came to me.

I'd packed up camp and went to relieve myself when I found something that confused and terrified the hell out of me. I went to piss by the tree where I buried the offal of the rabbit last night, and right where I'd buried them was a hole. It was rough, with long claw marks gouged deep into the dirt as if something had ripped into the ground to get what I'd buried.

I'd buried them deep enough to not attract the scent of wild animals, and I'd never seen claw marks like the ones next to the tree. I didn't know what to make of them; wild animals weren't that smart, and they were skittish by nature. No animal would risk getting close to a human unless they were starving, and no human had claws like the ones I'd found.

Without hesitation, I grabbed my rifle and racked a cartridge. I was petrified. I walked the camp in a circle, spreading out, searching for any tracks or signs. The only ones I'd found were some deer tracks about a hundred yards from camp that were at least a day old. There was nothing else even remotely resembling the marks I'd found.

There was nothing for me to find, and even though I was freaked out, I still had to hike back to civilization. As the miles wore on, I began to rationalize the experience, thinking it to be nothing more than a hungry animal looking for food and brave enough to sneak into my camp. I just hadn't buried the offal deep enough and some critter had smelled it. That's all it was.

I managed to bag another rabbit, purely on coincidence as it scampered out of the tree line. After the rabbit was clean, I wrapped the meat in cloth and stowed it away. I was hungry from the hike, and the fact that my breakfast had been stolen that morning, but I still wanted to put some more miles under my boots before it got dark.

As the sunlight faded from the canopy and my aching feet demanded a break, I found a spot to set up camp. It was a small campsite, nestled up against a rocky mound that stretched skyward for a couple of dozen feet with a slanted shelf near the top. I felt comfortable having my back to the wall, and a brace of trees next to the rock ensured I could set up my hammock.

I readied the campsite, built a roaring fire twice as large as the one last night just to scare away any nearby animals, and cooked the rabbit to perfection. I was ravenous and scarfed down the meat with gusto. Despite my hunger, there were still plenty of leftovers again, but this time, I was careful to stow the meat inside my pack, which I kept next to my hammock.

Exhaustion had worn me down from the many miles I'd walked that day, and I was eager to get some sleep. I laid my head on my pillow and was out like a light.

The stillness woke me, like a veil of silence had been draped over the woods. Not a single sound rose from the forest floor other than the rustling of the leaves in the wind. Not even crickets. Animals instinctively go quiet in the presence of predators, but this was unlike anything I'd ever felt before. I lay in my hammock, straining my ears to listen to any sound I could.

The fire had died out, leaving only coals that sparked every time a stiff breeze rolled in. The moon was fat in the sky and gave me ample light to see by as I stared up at the trees. For some reason, I was terrified to get up and look around. My rifle was next to me, resting just by [my] head against the tree. I could grab it in seconds and there was a round in the chamber, but I couldn't reach for my gun, couldn't do anything other than stare straight ahead and try not to move an inch. Because I realized something was watching me.

It's hard to describe the feeling. I knew what it was on a primal level, something instinctual, right alongside the fear of being alone in the dark. I knew that feeling too. The presence persisted for a few minutes and didn't fade. Sweat poured down my neck as I fought to stay still. Eventually, the silence and fear got to me, and I had to do something. I couldn't take it anymore and leaped from the hammock, hitting the ground hard. I ignored the pain radiating from my arms and scrambled for my rifle, scanning all around me, trying to find whatever it was.

As I spun around, I saw it, perched on the rocks above me. For a single split second, a flash of neon blue eyes stared back at me from an angular, too pale body before it slunk out of sight.

My heart pounded in my chest and my head felt fuzzy. It became hard to breathe and I fought to keep from passing out. I was scared out of my mind because whatever that thing had been, wasn't human, and it wasn't an animal. It was a monster.

I didn't sleep that night, I built up the fire and huddled around it, clutching my rifle until morning. Screw tradition and screw these woods. I was heading back to the cabin at first light, and I wasn't stopping till I reached it.

Nothing else happened through the night, but as dawn broke over the mountains, my nerves were shot to hell and my eyes ached with the strain of keeping them open. I stumbled to my feet, kicked out the fire, and slung my backpack over my shoulder. I left the hammock tied where it was and set off towards the stream. I was going to follow it to the trail, and I'd be back at the cabin well before nightfall.

It took an hour of walking, stumbling over uneven terrain until I found the stream, and from there I found the worn trail. I followed it for hours as the sun rose high in the sky. I was so tired, but the fear of death and that monster were the only things that kept me putting one foot in front of the other.

I was hungry, thirsty and beyond everything else, utterly exhausted. But I kept pushing forward, no matter how slow and tired I was. I still had the rabbit tied up in my pack, but I couldn't stop and eat. As the day wore on, I began to recognize parts of the terrain and I knew I was close to the cabin.

I was so elated that I didn't pay attention to where I was walking and rolled my ankle on a small rock that jutted out from the side of the trail. I lost my balance and careened off and hit my head on a nearby tree branch. Everything went black.

I awoke to dusk. I'd been out for a couple of hours, whether from the blow to the head or the exhaustion, whichever it was, I was still in the woods, and the night was coming quickly.

The monster never appeared during the daytime, so I thought I was safe in the light. But the light was running out and I still had a mile or so until I reached the cabin. I picked myself off the ground and dusted the dirt off. I grabbed my rifle, checked that it was still loaded, and I flicked the safety off. My finger stood a millimeter from the trigger, and I kept my head on a swivel as I hastily jogged the trail back to the cabin.

Relief swept through me when I saw the wraparound porch come into view. I had made it back. 'Dad!' I yelled as I ran up on the porch. 'Dad, we gotta go!'

I ran around to the front door and stood stock still as my blood ran cold.

The door to the cabin was open, and my dad was lying halfway inside and halfway on the porch. He'd been mauled. His body was nothing but ribbons and scraps of flesh that only half resembled what a human should look like.

I stared in silence, my mind not comprehending what I was seeing. He'd been wearing the red and black checked flannel shirt I'd gotten him for his birthday, it was the only way I could tell it was my dad. His face had been ripped from his skull; too white bone peeked out from his empty eye sockets.

The stench was ungodly; a mixture of fresh meat and the iron tang of blood filled the air. I clutched at my stomach and hurled bile on the wooden floorboards, sinking to my knees as my throat burned raw as I heaved my guts out.

Absolute panic gripped my sanity and took it for a joyride as I tried and failed to come to terms with the fact that my father was dead, had been ripped to pieces by whatever was outside, stalking me in the dark.

I had to leave, had to get as far away from that place as I could, or else, I'd be next. I screamed wordlessly and backed away from the porch. I turned and ran to the truck; it was my only avenue of escape and I had to hurry. Night had already fallen.

I scrambled [to] the driver's side of the pickup and yanked on the handle hard enough to break it, but it held and opened the door after a second of sticking. I climbed into the cab and threw down the vizor, where my dad usually kept the keys, but they weren't there. The only other place they could be was in the pocket of my dad's jeans. And I would have to get them.

Steeling myself for the inevitable, I clutched my rifle tight and exited the vehicle. I knew I had to be fast, knew I needed to already be far away from the woods, but my feet wouldn't carry me any further. I stared at the mutilated remains of my father and tried not to throw up again or break down in madness.

I squinted through my eyelashes and patted my dad's pants. The keys were in his left pocket, so as quickly as I could, I stepped to the side and dug through them. My hands clutched around the metal key, and I yanked my prize free, nearly stumbling from the force. With the key in my hand, I bolted from the porch back to the truck.

As I reached the open cab, something thudded against the wood and I turned, searching for the sound. Movement from above me drew my gaze and I finally got a good look at what had been chasing me through these godforsaken woods.

It was on the roof of the cabin, clinging to the side of the slanted roof with ease. The monster was a humanoid, but it crawled on all fours like an animal. Its skin was pale white like paper and thick and rough, leathery almost. But what marked it as being something inhuman was its head. It bore ethereal blue eyes that lit up the night, and a large, angular face that tapered to a point near its mouth. Its mouth opened, revealing thousands of minuscule, needlepoint, silver teeth in rows stretching down its throat.

The creature's eyes never left mine and glinted with malicious intelligence. It upturned its too many teeth into a gruesome smile. I didn't think, didn't panic, I just reacted. I raised my rifle and fired.

The bullet whizzed past its head and took it in the shoulder. Bright white blood spurted from the wound and splashed across the roof of the cabin to drip down the shingles. It let out a high-pitched shriek of pain and recoiled from the shock, it slid down the roof and into the tree line faster than I could line up a second shot. When it broke from my line of sight, I sprinted to the truck, tossed in my bag and rifle, and slid into the driver's seat.

Thankfully, the truck started on the first try, and the engine roared to life. I flicked on the high beams, threw the truck in reverse, and spun around as fast as I could. I was driving recklessly, taking curves too sharply and doing everything in my power not to fishtail into a tree when a thud landed on the roof of the truck, crumpling the aging metal.

I screeched, panicked, and jerked the wheel, trying to throw it off. I spun the wheel too much and clipped an overgrown tree in the process. I tried to overcorrect myself but only ended up slamming the side of the truck into the tree line.

The truck crunched to a halt, the passenger side crumpling like a bent can as tree branches snapped, sounding wooden gunshots through the forest. Whatever was on the truck was flung to the side as we crashed. It flew off the hood and hit a tree further into the forest. Bones cracked and when it fell to the dirt, it left a smear of white blood across the bark. I tried to start the truck again, but it just groaned and wouldn't turn over.

With a half growl, half groan, the creature picked its bleeding body off the ground and glared at me, its neon eyes glowing even brighter as it shrieked and crawled toward me.

I grabbed my rifle and left the truck. I could follow the

monster by its eyes alone and I perched my rifle on the hood of the truck and took aim.

It was slow as it crept toward me, giving me plenty of time to line up the perfect shot. I had my crosshairs centered right between its eyes and I rested my finger on the trigger, a split second away from firing. The creature let out another scream, much higher in pitch than the others and my body jerked of its own accord. My hands spasmed and I squeezed the trigger. My shot went wide, flying off into the woods and thudding into an old tree.

That had been my last bullet. My rifle only held four shots and I hadn't brought any extra ammo. I squeezed the trigger, again and again. Terror gripped me as it slunk along with the earth, leaving a milk-white trail of blood behind it. I threw the gun at it and ran for the truck, for the knife in my bag.

I wasn't going to let it get me, I wasn't going to end up as food, like a mutilated corpse – like my dad. I was going to kill it or myself if that failed. I wouldn't let it eat me.

The thing was on me before I reached the cab. It slammed into the side of the door, pinning me as I was halfway in the door. I lunged for my bag as the monster opened its jaws wide and bit through the metal door like it was cardboard. It ripped a chunk free and spat it on the ground as it eyed me with rage and hunger.

My hand closed around my bag, and I tore the strings, grabbing the knife that was at the top of the bag. I slid it from its sheath as the creature was poised to bite. I jammed the knife to the hilt in the side of its face, just below its glowing blue eye.

It reared back in pain, sending a mind-pounding shriek of pain splitting through my psyche. It stopped my heartbeat for a second as it jumped away from the truck and tried to dislodge the knife stuck in its skull.

I thought then that I'd landed a lucky blow and it was going to leave, that I'd be able to get back in the truck and escape the forest, but more howls joined the first and two more of the monsters slunk from out of the shadows.

This is where I die. It was the only thought running through my head. I couldn't run from them, couldn't fight them. I was going to die. But I wasn't going to make it easy for them.

I grabbed my torn bag, and I ran into the woods as fast as I could. I was desperate to escape, but the howls and thuds of too many legs padding through the dirt behind me told me I wouldn't escape.

They were close at my heels, and the only thing that saved my life that night was gravity and my clumsiness.

I tripped on a branch and tumbled to the ground as one of them sailed over me, mouth wide as a thousand needles closed around empty air. It hit the ground a few feet away and turned, eying me up. I backpedaled but hit a tree as it lunged a second time.

With nothing else in my hands, I brought my bag up as it clamped down, throwing me to the forest floor. Its teeth closed around my bag, ripping the nylon to shreds, but my mini shovel got lodged in its throat and it couldn't close its mouth all the way. Clothing and food poured out of its jaws, and I scrambled out from under it.

My hand hit something plastic as I crawled away from the creature and even in the dark of the woods, I couldn't fail to make out the bright orange handle of the flare gun.

It was a long shot, but it was the last weapon I had, and I clung to it as I stood up and ran away. I didn't get far as the monster chomped through the metal shovel like it was a toothpick and spat out the remains of my backpack. It howled in rage and ran for me. Knowing I only had one shot, I stopped running, dropped to my knees, and fired.

Daylight split the night as my eyesight was obliterated by the burning red flare as it streaked through the air and hit the monster in the face. Like it'd been doused in kerosene, the creature went up in a gulf of flames. Its flesh sizzled and popped like grease in a pan as it cracked and blackened in seconds. It howled in agony, screaming such a high-pitched sound that my ears bled, and I fell to my knees as my consciousness waned.

By the time I rose to my feet and wiped the blood from my ears, it was dead. It was now nothing but a charred carcass burning under the crackling fire. The flare still burned, illuminating the night. And showing me the other two creatures that had crept upon us.

I was out of weapons and out of hope, but they stayed back, just at the tree line, watching me and the flaming carcass of their friend. The fire was their weakness it seemed, and even though I had no more flares, I bluffed them. It was the most reckless thing I could've done, but I had no other options left. I raised the empty flare gun, and they flinched. They took a step back and stayed low to the ground like they were ready to bolt.

I pressed my luck and took a step forward. They turned and ran as fast as they could, deeper into the forest, howling as they did so.

As soon as they were out of sight, I ran myself. I ran as fast as my legs would carry me, not caring about the scrapes and scratches from the branches whipping at my face. I only cared about my survival.

I hit the road leading to the highway and ran for hours.

There were too many miles between me and the highway, but I didn't care. I just kept running.

By the time I hit the pavement, it was daybreak, and I knew I could stop running, but I kept on. Because I had nothing else but the run. If I stopped, it would mean accepting what just happened, and I didn't think my mind would survive.

I ran until I hit the gas station we'd stopped at only three days ago, what felt like a lifetime ago. The gas station attendant took one look at me, out of breath, with bloody, torn clothing, and called the police.

He was kind enough to give me all the water I wanted while we waited for the police. I drank it in silence while I sat huddled in on myself, trying to calm my racing heart and not to think.

It took the cops nearly an hour to arrive from the nearest town, and when they did, I finally had to tell them my story.

They didn't believe me, because of course they wouldn't. I sounded insane, raving about monsters with glowing blue eyes and white blood like a madman. However, the officer was patient and kind, taking down my statement word for word, despite the skepticism on his face.

I told them where to find the cabin, the truck, everything.

They found it all right where I told them it would be, but there was no sign of the creature I'd killed, not even ashes. My dad's body was also gone. The only sign it had been there at all was the bloodstains.

The police chalked it up to a wild animal attack, attributing my story to be just that, a story by a scared teenager who witnessed an animal kill his father. The reporters, the kids at school, hell, even my mother, they didn't believe me.

But I know the truth. I'm not crazy. There's something evil in that forest.

Whatever it was.

There's more than one of them, and they burn just fine.

If you camp out in the Tennessee forests at night, be careful, learn from my story. And for the love of God, carry a fire source." EU

I questioned EU about the authenticity of the events he described in the account. I was told, by EU, that his father did die under the circumstances detailed in the narrative.

I was asked not to disclose any names or locations, but I was given specified information to verify the story.

As far as I can tell, through my own investigation, this incident did occur. Do I believe that some "creative writing" was included in the narrative? Absolutely. But I have no reason to believe that EU has fictionalized this tragedy.

Many researchers of the paranormal (including myself) believe that some manifestations and poltergeist phenomena (objects flying, doors slamming, etc.) are products of the human mind (tulpas or thought-form manifestation).

To test that idea, a fascinating experiment was conducted in the early 1970s by the Toronto Society for Psychical Research (TSPR) to see if they could create a "ghost." The idea was to assemble a group of people who would make up a completely fictional character and then, through séances, see if they could contact him, receive messages and other physical phenomena. Perhaps even create an apparition.

Dr. A. R. G. Owen led a group of eight people from the Toronto Society for Psychical Research. None of these people were known to have any abilities in ESP, psychic, channeling, or other physical or mental specialties. They proceeded to create a person on paper, giving the person the name Philip Aylesford.

The group created Philip's entire life story: He lived in seventeenth-century England, was married, had a love affair, and ultimately died by his hand in 1654. A member of the group even traveled to England to photograph the area it was said Philip had lived. Another group member sketched a drawing of Mr. Aylesford. The experiment began with the entire group meeting frequently to discuss the life and times of Philip as they would any exceptional real person.

After a year of continued experimentation, Philip began to make "his" presence known. Beginning with simple taps and raps to questions. He even gave factual answers to known historical events of his time. Soon after, Philip manifested physical abilities. He was able to shake and move a table the group used.

The experiment was conducted several times with different groups of people and was able to create other manifestations, including Lilith, an eighteenth-century French-Canadian spy; Sebastian, a medieval alchemist; and Axel, a man from the future. All manifested very quickly after the experiment started and communicated via raps and taps. At the beginning of the experiment, the stated goal was to eventually create an apparition. Though toward the end of 1977 the group felt they were close to reaching that goal, interest in the experiment eventually waned, and activities were discontinued.

That being stated, can meme humanoids and other entities be digitally created by humans, then unconsciously manifested into a physical form? Have we reached a point to where we can create "mind monsters" that could perpetuate our demise? I suppose we'll be able to answer those questions eventually.

ABOUT THE AUTHOR

Lon Strickler is a Fortean researcher, author, and publisher of the syndicated 'Phantoms and Monsters' blog. He began the blog in 2005, which has steadily grown in popularity and is read daily by tens of thousands of paranormal enthusiasts, investigators and those seeking the truth. His research and reports have been featured on hundreds of online media sources. Several of these published reports have been presented on various television segments, including The History Channel's 'Ancient Aliens,' Syfy's 'Paranormal Witness', 'Fact or Faked: Paranormal Files,' and Destination America's 'Monsters and Mysteries in America.'

He has been interviewed on hundreds of radio & online broadcasts, including multiple guest appearances on 'Coast to

Coast AM.' He was also featured on Destination America's 'Monsters and Mysteries in America' television show for 'The Sykesville Monster' episode. Lon has written 9 books and is currently the host of Phantoms & Monsters Radio.

Lon was born and raised in south central Pennsylvania, near the Gettysburg National Military Park and Battlefield. After living in the Baltimore, MD metro area for 40 years, he eventually moved back to his hometown in 2016.

ALSO BY LON STRICKLER

Mothman Dynasty: Chicago's Winged Humanoids

Alien Disclosure: Experiencers Expose Reality

Winged Cryptids: Humanoids, Monsters &
Anomalous Creatures Casebook

Printed in Great Britain
by Amazon